"I FEEL LIKE A VENDING MACHINE . . ." Jim Conway writes, describing his own mid-life crisis in the midst of a successful pastorate. "Someone pushes a button, and out comes a sermon. Someone pushes another button, and out comes a magazine article. The family pushes buttons, and out comes dollars or time-involvement. The community pushes other buttons, and I show up for meetings, sign petitions, and take stands."

The male mid-life crisis is for real. "To many men it seems that from 40 on is all downhill," Conway explains. "They still have 25 to 30 good, productive years left, and yet they are asking, 'Where do I go from here?' "

Some men go to the arms of a younger woman; others quit their jobs and try a whole new life-style. The ones who hang on to their commitments are still battered by a hurricane of fears, self-doubts, and frustrations.

While others have described the problem, this is the book that moves on to solutions. Jim Conway is still at his church . . . still married to the same woman . . . and has written this guidebook to help men, their wives, and their children weather the storm by holding on to a God who doesn't condemn but always sustains.

Mary E. Anderson

MEN IN MID LIFE CRISIS

JIM CONWAY

David C. Cook Publishing Co.

ELGIN, ILLINOIS—WESTON, ONTARIO

First printing, December 1978
Eleventh printing, June 1981

Scripture quotations, unless otherwise noted, are from the Living
Bible.

Edited by Ronald Wilson and Dean Merrill
Designed by Kurt Dietsch
Photos by Jim Whitmer
Printed in the United States of America

ISBN: 0-89191-145-6
Library of Congress Catalog Number: 78-67098

To my wife, Sally,
Who for this book has been my
    Researcher,
    Editor,
    Typist, and
    Friendly Critic;
And who for all of our marriage has been my
    Encourager,
    Lover, and
    Closest Friend.

CONTENTS

FOREWORD

Born out of the crucible of personal experience, this book brings front and center a problem evangelicals have previously ignored. With candor, insight, sensitivity, and compassion, Pastor Conway explores the multicausal complexity of this life-upsetting trauma. But he does far more than trace the roots of mid-life crises. He offers concrete, tested counsel from Scripture, psychology, and his own ministry.

More than that, he holds out realistic assurance that a man can emerge from his struggle with self-doubt, vocational despair, and existential darkness a stronger, deeper person who in human weakness has discovered the resources of God's power.

VERNON GROUNDS
President
Conservative Baptist Seminary
Denver, Colorado

April, 1978

NOT ALL
THE KING'S HORSES . . .

MY DEPRESSION HAD GROWN all through the spring, summer, and fall. By October it had reached giant proportions. I would often stare out the window or simply sit in a chair, gazing into space. Several times I had gone for long drives in the car, on bike rides, or on long walks. I had literally come to the bottom of me. I was ready to chuck everything. Repeatedly I had fantasies of getting on a sailboat and sailing off to some unknown destination where no one knew me and where I carried no responsibility for anyone in my church or my family.

By mid-November the depression had grown to unbelievable proportions. Since spring, my wife, Sally, and I had been researching this book. I had hoped that by taking off November I could spend a great deal of time on the final draft, but now I was ready to throw everything away.

On a cold, wintry night, I went for a long walk and made some decisions. I would resign as pastor of the church, write a letter to Fuller Seminary to tell them I was dropping my doctoral program, and write to my publishers to tell them I no longer would be writing. I would also legally turn everything over to Sally, take only our 1968 Cutlass, and start driving south. For me, it was all over. I had had it with people, with responsibility, with society, even with God, who had been such a close friend all of my adult life. He seemed now to be distant and remote, uninterested in the agony through which I was going.

You see, this book is about me as well as other men in mid-life. I felt like the proverbial Humpty Dumpty who had just come crashing off the wall, and all the king's horses and all the king's men couldn't possibly put my life back together. All I could do was cry in desperation a psalm I had learned many years ago:

> Come, Lord, and show me your mercy, for I am helpless, overwhelmed, in deep distress; my problems go from bad to worse. Oh, save me from them all! See my sorrows; feel my pain; forgive my sins. (Ps. 25:16-18)

PART

1 IT'S FOR REAL

1
THE CRISIS

I HAD NOT PREVIOUSLY MET the woman sitting across the desk from me. She had been referred by another woman whose husband was going through mid-life crisis. She had hardly introduced herself before she began to cry with great convulsive sobs. It was as if I were watching a person disintegrate before my eyes.

After several minutes she looked up, mascara running down over her puffy cheeks, the hair around her face wet with tears, a clump of wadded Kleenex in her lap. The story about her confusing relationship with her husband poured out.

They were now married more than fifteen years. All this time he had been an ideal husband and father. He had been kind, thankful, gentle, and thoughtful. He enjoyed spending time with the children. He was a man oriented to his career, moving steadily toward his ultimate goal of being a congressman.

Then the change came. He had taken a short-term job in another state, and the family had joined him for the summer. When the summer ended and it was time for the family to go home, the wife began to realize that he was not simply sending them home; he was sending them away. A number of changes in his personality followed. He couldn't stand being around his wife or being touched by her. Almost anything she said made him angry. He felt he was being exploited and misunderstood by his family. It was as though everything in his life had suddenly gone sour.

Some days after his wife saw me, he came to my office, suspicious and fearing that I as a pastor-counselor might heap guilt upon him and scold him for the change in his life. As he began to trust me, he shared that nothing really seemed worthwhile anymore. He didn't appear to be moving fast enough toward his career goal; his marriage was tasteless and dull; and the tennis he had taken up was only a momentary diversion from the oppressive boredom of his life.

The only thing that seemed to give life to him was a young woman whom he had met. She was in her twenties; she seemed able to take him back to his own twenties. They did new things together—picnicking, lying out under the stars, and walking along the beach. She read poetry to him. And her touch—it made him feel so alive! She was so warm and real. She understood him. They could talk about all kinds of things. He felt so free, so good, as if life finally had meaning again. Sex was not a duty or a chore; it was exhilarating and life-giving.

I asked him why he had come to see me—apparently this new love was providing all of the things he wanted in life. He then shared the other part of his life—his children. He couldn't forget them. He wanted to be their father; he wanted to be with them. The trouble was his wife—if only he could have the children and get rid of his wife. That would solve all of his problems.

Over the following months there were short times of separation, but always he found himself inexorably drawn back to his family. He was exhilarated when he was with his girlfriend, yet he seemed to need the ties with his wife and family. Here was a man, as the song says, "torn between two lovers, feeling like a fool." He was torn between two lives, two life-styles, two directions, two ages. Here was a man in mid-life crisis.

DANGER AHEAD

The man approaching mid-life has some strange and difficult times ahead of him. He may negotiate the walk along the unfamiliar top of the brick wall with little trouble, but many men in mid-life feel more like Humpty Dumpty.

The mid-life crisis is a time of high risk for marriages. It's a time of possible career disruption and extramarital affairs. There is depression, anger, frustration, and rebellion The crisis is a pervasive thing that seems to affect not only the physical but also the social, cultural, spiritual, and occupational expressions of a man's life.

It is a time when a man reaches the peak of a mountain range. He looks back over where he has come from and forward to what lies ahead. He also looks at himself and asks, "Now that I've climbed the mountain, am I any different for it? Do I feel fulfilled? Have I achieved what I wanted to achieve?"

How he evaluates his past accomplishments, hopes,

and dreams will determine whether his life ahead will be an exhilarating challenge to him or simply a demoralizing distance that must be drearily traversed. In either case, he is at a time of trauma, because his emotions, as never before, are highly involved.

OPPORTUNITY ALSO

The Chinese have a picture-word for crisis. The lines of the combination symbol indicate opportunity as well as danger.

CRISIS   DANGER   OPPORTUNITY

This crisis in a man's life is really an opportunity to realize more fully all of the potentials of his personality. A woman in mid-life says optimistically, "[Now] we are able to confront reality, to look again, to strip away many pretenses that may have stopped us from living the way we want to, and to change our life while we still have time left ahead of us to live it."[1]

HE'S A PIONEER

In the 1930s Walter Pitkin made publishing history with a best-seller, *Life Begins at Forty*, which introduced a new era in life. It was not until this century that many people began to live through what we now call the middle years. In prehistoric times man lived an average of about eighteen years. Fossil remains indicate that only a few lived beyond forty. Even as recently as 1900, life expectancy was about forty-eight for a man and fifty-one for a woman. In 1900 only 10 percent of the population was "middle-aged." Today the average adult person in the labor force is over forty-five. Our total population has increased almost 100 percent in the last century, but middle-agers have increased over 200 percent.

We are dealing with a developmental crisis in American life and history that is relatively new and may, in many ways, be unique to our culture. Dr. Jack Weinberg, clinical director of the Illinois Psychiatric Institute, believes "that the mid-life transition is more a problem for Americans than for other nationalities, because of the nature of our society. We're hard-driving, success-oriented, future-oriented people. We reward youth and pragmatism and productivity. We mete out insults, conscious and unconscious, to the middle-aged and aging."[2]

HE AWAKENS TO A SURPRISE

A man in mid-life has crossed a cultural barrier that influences the way he is viewed at work, by his family, and in society in general. Much is known about childhood, teenage, and young-adult development, and libraries are loaded with books on gerontology. Unfortunately, there seems to be an absence of information about the adult in the long era between the early twenties and retirement. The person in mid-life is surprised by a developmental crisis he was not expecting, and there is little written material to help him.

In the early fifties Dr. Edmund Bergler, one of the pioneers in exposing man's mid-life crisis in *The Revolt of the Middle-Aged Man*, recorded a comment from a wife who was surprised by the drastic change in her husband. "I believe that my husband is either disintegrating or going crazy. My husband has always been a reliable, satisfied, solid person, with a good sense of humor, and a sense of duty. All at once, in the last few months, his whole personality has changed. All he does is rebel and attack. He attacks marriage, myself, even his profession. He is rambunctious, cantankerous, unruly, practically unmanageable. I don't know for sure, but I suspect there is a girl. His constant furies and his attacks on everybody and everything seem to use up all his energy. At least as far as I am concerned. There is nothing he approves of anymore."[3]

HIS INNER FEELINGS

There is no sudden biological event that causes these emotional changes, nothing, at least, comparable to the female menopause. A man does, however, have some of the same feelings common to menopause—depression, anxiety, irritability, fatigue, self-pity, and overall unhappiness with life.

In the play *Herzog* by Saul Bellow we can catch the feeling of the man in mid-life crisis. Herzog is overcome with a desperate need to explain life and put it into perspective. He begins to consider the value of his entire life and concludes that he has mismanaged everything and that his life is literally ruined. He sees himself as having failed with both of his wives, his son and daughter, his parents, his country, his brothers and sisters, his friends, and even his own soul. Previously, the occupations of living life had kept him busy, but now his life is disintegrating into hopeless despair.

As another man put it, "If I had my life to live over again, I'd be a failure. I'd be better off, because then I wouldn't have as much to lose as I do now."[4] Or, as Byron expressed it in his poem, "On This Day I Complete My Thirty-Sixth Year":

> My days are in the yellow leaf;
>   The flowers and fruits of Love are gone;
> The worm, the canker, and the grief
>   Are mine alone!

It seems, as you talk to men and women in their forties, you get the distinct impression that the men are far more unhappy than the women. Women seem to be a bit more future-oriented, whereas men in the middle of life seem to feel that the best was in the past.

Our society quite clearly lays out the path that the young adult male is expected to follow. He should marry, establish a home, get started in a career, then move up the ladder of success. By age forty many men have accomplished all of these goals, and so it seems that from forty on is all downhill. They still have twenty-five to thirty good, productive years left, and yet they are asking, "Where do I go from here if, in fact, all that society has expected me to accomplish has already been done?"

HE'S DEPRESSED

Depression is one of two major emotional feelings prevalent to the man in mid-life. True depression incapacitates a person. He feels worthless and hopeless, often complaining of fatigue and experiencing real or imaginary physical disorders.

A man is caught in a situation where he feels there are no answers or solutions. He is like a rabbit caught in a trap, with the options of waiting for the hunter to come to nab him or of chewing off his own leg and escaping into life maimed. The hopelessness of the choices causes him to be intensely depressed, immobilized by fear, to distort reality and react in irrational panic.

MAGNIFICENT MARTYR

Self-pity is the second predominant theme. When the TV show "Male Menopause" examined the mid-life crisis, John J. O'Connor, television critic for *The New York Times*, commented on the program, "The monotonous tone throughout is one of self-pity."[5]

The man at mid-life feels sorry for himself because he thinks he is a trapped man. He must now act his age. He is bound to duty. He is tied to a treadmill. He provides for his family and fills innumerable positions in society. Yet he is the target of indignation, nagged to do his duties, and all of the time he is unable to tell anyone that he is desperately bewildered inside. He wonders what hit him and if life is worth living. He may finally rebel against all of this and abandon the two things he perceives to be causing the problem—his wife and his work. He will later learn that abandoning these was not a good solution and will return from disillusionment with a giant martyr complex and self-pity written across his forehead in neon lights.

TRAPPED IN SILENCE

Several years ago *The New York Times* ran an anonymous letter which read in part, "I was forty years old and my husband forty-six when the eccentric behavior began. An otherwise reasonable and family-loving man suffered, not depression as we understood it, but rage, fatigue, incommunicability, suspicion, hostility. But every incident was my fault supposedly; I was the woman and I was alleged to be in the change of life. . . . Unfortunately, doctors, psychiatrists, *men in general, have kept it all under the rug where they have swept it themselves.* They are in terror of the truth of acknowledging a condition which affects their behavior beyond their control, but which they readily ascribe to women without mercy. . . ." (Italics mine.)

It is extremely painful for a man to talk about his problems. Over the years women have been the first ones to come to my office to get help with a marital problem. The wife has had to encourage her husband to seek outside help. He is always the one dragging his feet. Our culture conditions men not to share their troubles. They are the leaders. They are strong. They are not supposed to cry, feel pain or hurt; they are not supposed to be frustrated, confused, or disappointed with life. To admit that there is a problem many times destroys that quality of "man" within him. The man in mid-life crisis would rather grin and bear it—tough it out. He would rather take his lumps than to share with anyone.

This silence is tragic. Vachel Lindsay's poem "The Leaden-Eyed" is quoted by Eda LeShan: ". . .not that they die, but that they die like sheep. . . ." LeShan reflects, "I think what I heard too often in my talks with middle-aged men was the bleating of sheep."[6]

It's time for men to stop rolling over and playing dead, or walking off silently to the slaughter of mid-life crisis. They need to share their feelings with people around them, with each other, and with God. It's time for Christians in general and the church in particular to acknowledge that there is a developmental crisis of giant proportions that needs sympathetic understanding and support from the community of believers.

AWARENESS IS A BEGINNING

Not only are men unwilling to talk about the mid-life crisis, but they may not realize what is happening, or they may deliberately ignore it or, even worse, reject the reality that aging is taking place. A saying goes, "A young man lives through his body, an old man lives against it."

The mid-life developmental transition is intertwined with all of a man's life—everything he's done and thought in the past and everything he will do and think and become in the future. It will not go away simply by being ignored or rejected. A man is not the same person he was at twenty-five, nor are his cultural surroundings the same. Someone put it another way, "We spend about one-quarter of our lives growing up and three-quarters growing old."[7]

Instead of ignoring or rejecting the mid-life crisis, it should be viewed as perhaps the most exciting time in life. I agree with the authors who wrote, "No other decade is more intriguing, complex, interesting, and *un*-settled. Its characteristics are change, flux, crisis, growth and intense challenges. Other than childhood, no period has a greater impact on the balance of our lives, for at no other time is anxiety coupled with so great a possibility for fulfillment."[8]

HE IS NOT ALONE

Because men do not share their feelings, they are unaware that other men at this age are having a similar struggle. The truth is that nearly all men in mid-life experience some trauma. At one point or another they all feel like a fallen Humpty Dumpty, smashed and forever beyond repair. The degree of intensity and duration of time may vary, but the crisis comes to the white-collar worker and the blue-collar worker, to the married and the single, *and* to the Christian and to the unbeliever. The crisis has been documented by experts, observed by counselors and psychoanalysts, and experienced by multitudes (probably all) of modern American men. A man must face it frankly if he is to find any hope or help for the future.

> Show me the path where I should go, O Lord; point out the right road for me to walk. Lead me; teach me; for you are the God who gives me salvation. I have no hope except in you. (Ps. 25:4-5)

2
EXPERT OPINIONS

IT IS TREMENDOUSLY ENCOURAGING that an increasing number of specialists in the area of adult development have begun to explore the problems of men in mid-life. In the seventies a rash of magazine and newspaper articles appeared, beginning to explain that there is a real problem and that all men in mid-life need some help.

WHEN DOES THE CRISIS COME?

Experts disagree on what years should be identified as the mid-years or when the crisis is most likely to take place. Kenn Rogers says that his studies show that the crisis appears between age thirty and thirty-nine.[1] Carl Jung places the height of the mid-life trauma between thirty-five and forty.[2] Joel and Lois Davitz say it occurs between forty and fifty, the peak age being age forty-five.[3] Barbara Fried also places the crisis in the forties.[4] In 1968 Lee Stockford presented findings based on three studies involving more than 2,100 men and women. His research indicated that 80 percent of the executives aged thirty-four to forty-two were hit by this crisis.[5] Dr. Daniel Levinson, a Yale researcher who has been involved in an extensive study of the mid-life male, puts the mid-life decade at thirty-five to forty-five.[6] Gail Sheehy in *Passages* echoes Levinson's view.[7] Others, however, put the mid-life reevaluation time in the fifties.

In a real sense, the mid-life crisis is not so much a matter of a man's chronological age as it is his state of mind. The kinds of goals he has chosen and how he has handled earlier developmental problems helps determine whether he will arrive early or late at the mid-life crisis.

IS THERE A MALE MENOPAUSE?

People have suggested that since men experience the similar emotions of self-pity, gloom, unhappiness, depression, and irritability that a woman feels as she goes through menopause, perhaps there is some hormonal change in men: a male menopause. The evidence we have says no. There is no common biological change in a man that causes this emotional change. If, however, we are talking about "male menopause" as a "turning point," then such a thing does take place, according to Daniel Levinson.[8]

However, men are so sure they are not going to experience the drastic biological change of life that they have a false sense of security, unaware that a crisis will come aside from a biological upheaval.

SECOND CHILDHOOD

The man who is not expecting anything to happen to him as he moves along through life is startled to find that in mid-life he begins to act somewhat like an adolescent. He finds himself now acting in the same bizarre ways as his teenage child.

Reassessment is the prevailing theme of the mid-life crisis. He is asking questions about values, who he is, what he wants to be, what his work is, what he is accomplishing. He is asking questions about his marriage, job, friendships, social commitments, and himself. These are the same kinds of questions his teenager is asking: "Who am I? Who will I be? What will my values be? What will my life work be? Who will my friends be? Who will I marry? What part will God have in my life?"

THREE MAJOR FORCES

The mid-life crisis is not caused by a simple problem that can be resolved with a simplistic answer. It's not going to go away with two aspirins and a good night's sleep. Nor is it going to go away by simply telling the man to read his Bible more, believe God, and stop worrying.

Three major forces converge on the man at this time in his life.[9] First, some biological changes do take place. He is losing physical vigor and muscle tone, his body weight is shifting, and he is losing his hair. Death suddenly becomes more of a reality.

Secondly, his psychological makeup—his ego, his self-image—is affected. He begins to view himself as less of a man because his view of his self-worth stemmed from his physical strength. He may be having trouble or dissatisfaction at work, and because many men draw ego strength from what they accomplish, this may also hurt his self-image. He may think he's not the man he used to be. He may see that he's not going to meet all his goals, or, perhaps, he has met them and says, "So what?"

The third major area of his life being affected is his social life. The world in very clear tones tells him that there isn't meaningful life after forty and he can't get a job after forty-five or fifty. Television commercials continue to affirm that youth is good, age is bad. Because he feels rejected by society, he begins to reevaluate his life in social areas—his relationship to his wife, his children, his career, his colleagues, his friends, the world around him, and God.

THE CRISIS IS INEVITABLE

By now the picture may be so black and dismal that our hero is crying, "How in the world can I get out of this? Stop the merry-go-round and let me off." Or, "God, why in the world did you make us so that this kind of pressure would be our lot in life?"

There is a growing opinion among sociologists, psychologists, psychiatrists, and other professionals that all men are going to go through the crisis to some degree, and each will come through it with either a positive outlook for the future or a glum outlook marked by despair. It is a natural developmental crisis and, at the same time, it is unavoidable.

Escaping the mid-life developmental crisis is probably as likely as the child escaping adolescence. A teenager may put off facing this developmental phase, but sooner or later he must answer those questions of who he is and what he wants to do in life. The man in mid-life may suppress the reassessment of his life, but he must face it eventually.

Before the mid-life crisis, it is possible to think of yourself as young. After you have successfully dealt with the developmental problems of mid-life, you will be able to comfortably accept yourself as no longer young, but having a valuable contribution to make that the young cannot.

A DANGEROUS TIME FOR OTHERS

When the teenager is going through such an evaluation, his emotional gyrations, alternating directions, and changing values don't really affect many people other than his immediate family. He may decide to drop out, fool around with sex or drugs, put God on a shelf for a while, and he may become antisocial, irritable, and depressed. His parents, because they are older, a bit more secure, and understand what the adolescent is going through, are able to remain objective, cool, and collected in most situations. They realize that this is a passing phase, and soon the young person will emerge into young adulthood.

However, the man in the mid-life crisis who begins to do the same things as the teenager causes terrifying havoc in his family, his business, and his community.

For example, if he begins an extramarital affair, a great many futures hinge on what happens with that affair. He is no longer a teenager trying to learn a little bit about sex; he is now a man with a wife and children, who depend on his stability. He is a man who, perhaps, holds several positions in the community on various committees and boards. He is a man whose business or political future may be affected by the sexual affair.

The man in mid-life crisis has more social expertise, power, and freedom than the adolescent. For those reasons his hostility or rebellion may be extremely dangerous to every other person involved with him.

SOMETHING HAPPENED TO HIS CLOCK

Something is wrong with the clock for the man in the mid-life crisis. In fact, on many occasions he seems totally disoriented from time. We often generalize about people at different ages. Youth, for example, is thought to look more toward the future, ignoring the past. Grandparents, on the other hand, look backward. The man in the middle seems to be most concerned with *now*. When he looks to the future, he sees old age creeping in on him and the inevitability of death. He senses the cessation of work, productivity, influence, impact, and life itself. When he looks to the past, he sees only a long list of goals and dreams that have not been accomplished and that can never be accomplished, so he badly wants to live life now.

There is, however, another problem. He is often so preoccupied with his past failures and future fears that he is unable to enjoy the now. Even though he feels an urgency to make something happen before it is too late, he fails to enjoy life as it comes. He doesn't enjoy his wife and family, his work, God, or nature and creation.

FACT OR FANTASY

The pressure of time running out brings the facts of life into a brutal clash with the fantasies a man has dreamed since youth or young adulthood. "Someday" he was to become king of this or that; "someday" he was to be a millionaire, a sports hero, an actor or poet or singer or writer; "someday" he was going to be a great lover. "Someday" he was going to be—as my oldest daughter often says—"rich and famous." But suddenly *now* is upon him. He's reached mid-life—and he begins to realize that the future is here, that all he is ever going to achieve must happen now. It's got to happen by forty, or at least by forty-five.

His young-adult dreams and fantasies are confronted with the reality that he has a job, but he is never going to become boss or the president. He has a house in the suburbs, but he is never really going to be a millionaire. He can watch a lot of football on Sunday afternoon, but he is never really going to be a professional quarterback. He may have actually reached the top in his work and arrived at his goals, but he still isn't as happy as he thought he'd be. He comes for the first time to face the facts of his life and compare them to the fantasies that have motivated him over the past twenty years.

Dr. Ernest van den Haag, a psychoanalyst and a psychologist, says, "This crisis consists in the clash between your fantasies and reality. You begin to have a more realistic conception of yourself." Dr. van den Haag goes on to say that the difference between the crises in adolescence and in mid-life is that the adolescent has not tested his ability and is looking forward to the future with optimism to see his fantasies fulfilled. "When you have reached middle age, if you are realistic, you see the limitations of your career. And that is something that is for most people rather difficult to take."[10]

It is this very comparison of dreams versus the demonstrated accomplishments of life that causes men in the mid-life crisis to experience depression. Only as a man can successfully face the facts of who he is and what he can do, will he be able to graciously move to the next era in life.

SEARCH FOR A SPIRITUAL ANSWER

I've watched a number of men in mid-life crisis who not only have had their jobs and their relationships with their wife and children affected, but they have also come to a point of blaming God for what is taking place. Carl Jung found that the root of the mental illness among all his patients over the age of about thirty-five was a loss of spiritual moorings. It is heartbreaking for a man who has been a leader in the church and who has provided spiritual stability for young and old to suddenly, because of guilt, anger, depression, and confusion, throw God overboard. Throwing God away will only increase his sense of instability.

> I stand silently before the Lord, waiting for him to rescue me. For salvation comes from him alone. Yes, he alone is my Rock, my rescuer, defense and fortress. Why then should I be tense with fear when troubles come? (Ps. 62:1-2)

3
BELIEVE ME,
IT REALLY HAPPENS

I TOLD YOU EARLIER that I write as one who has experienced mid-life crisis. If you know something about me, this book may mean more to you.

WHAT I DO

I am the senior pastor of a large church on the edge of a university campus. I spend a lot of time counseling students and families in the church as well as people from outside our church. I contribute a monthly column to a magazine, answering emotional-spiritual questions of students, and I have pastored two other churches. I have two master's degrees and am working on a doctorate.

I am married to Sally, who loves me deeply and who

has made me more than I ever thought I could be. We have three daughters—Barbara and Brenda in college and Becky in high school. Our family enjoys traveling. We have vacationed in many parts of the United States, camping most of the time. Sally and I have been overseas three times for long periods to minister in different countries. Our three daughters accompanied us on one of the trips.

WHO I AM

The above doesn't really tell you too much about who I am inside, although you begin to get a picture as you see how I've spent time in my life.

I like people; I like to be needed; but I also enjoy being alone. I like the woods and the out-of-doors, except in winter. I like to see things grow. I am turned on by seeing the first sprouts of daffodils and tulips in the spring. I can sit for hours watching water, and I like to sail. We have a sixteen-foot catamaran, and I enjoy sailing when the wind is blowing hard and I'm able to fly one hull out of the water. I like the challenge of my skill against the unpredictableness of the wind.

I am a fairly creative person. I like to do unusual things in the church worship services to stimulate people into sensing the relevancy of God's involvement in our lives. (Sometimes I get into trouble by doing things that are too different.)

You also need to know that as a teen I had an extremely low self-image. In those years I felt as though I were unsuccessful in every area of life. Academically, I barely made it. Teachers graciously passed me along. There were 614 people in my high-school graduating class, and

I ranked below 600. The principal told my father that he shouldn't spend his money sending me to college, because I would never make it. My counselors advised me to go to trade school, where I could use my hands.

In high school I was a loner. I had very few friends, and those friends were older than I. I began to run track, hoping somehow to gain some measure of approval before somebody. Unfortunately, even in that area, I was not very successful. Every time I think of my adolescent years, I'm reminded of the story of the man who went to a psychiatrist and told him how inadequate he felt. He listed at length all of the areas that caused him to feel inferior. After his sad tale of woe, the psychiatrist looked at him and said, "Man, you don't just *feel* inadequate; you *are* inadequate!"

My life began to change drastically when I went to college. I had become a Christian shortly before, and God, through the Bible, began to bolster my self-image with promise after promise of his love, care, and direction. He showed me that "I can do everything God asks me to with the help of Christ who gives me the strength and power" (Phil. 4:13).

The second greatest thing that happened to me was meeting Sally, who loved me as I was and believed I could be more than I was. We were married after my graduation from college.

You should also know that I am a workaholic. I tend to work hard so that people will love me. Even though I have felt a definite call from God into full-time ministry, and I love to be God's servant doing his work, it's easy for me to be caught in a bind between seeking God's approval and man's approval.

I also tend to be very sensitive. I feel things very deeply, and it has only been the last five to seven years that I have begun to let my emotions show publicly.

Frequently I have been deeply touched while preaching and have become unable to speak. Several times I have broken down in tears. At first, these were very humiliating times for me, but I have come to see that it has helped other people, especially men, express their emotions.

WHY WRITE A BOOK ON THE MID-LIFE CRISIS?

That question was put to me by a colleague who said, "Here you are, pastoring a university church with young people around you all the time. You are writing for a youth magazine. It seems you ought to be writing a book on the college age." That may be true, and perhaps someday I will follow his suggestion, but I think you are beginning to see now that I am writing on the mid-life crisis not only for others' benefit but also for mine.

To me, the mid-life crisis isn't simply an academic problem. It isn't that I am a writer who is looking for a new book to write. I have been struggling with the whole mid-life crisis that came upon me as a very shocking experience, one for which I was totally unprepared. I had seen the problem in the lives of other people, but I never anticipated it would happen to me.

As I look back, I can remember my dad at about this age. He was also a workaholic, but he suddenly stopped working so much, and went out and bought an airplane. He learned to fly and would quite often leave work in the middle of the day to fly. At the time I thought he was only taking up a hobby, but I see in retrospect that he was going through a struggle in his life.

About the same time my dad's brother, a partner in their business, sold his half, sold his house, moved his family to Florida, and started in an entirely different line of business. It seemed he was saying that he was getting older, and life was too short to spend it all in cold, smoky Cleveland.

I look back to my seminary days and remember a pastor and his wife in their forties who were having trouble in their marriage. There were rumors of an affair; he later left the church; and there was a divorce. Today this gifted preacher is in the business world.

A number of friends of mine from college and seminary years are now going through the same kinds of mid-life struggles. Some of them are leaving their churches, some are going into new careers, and some have had problems with their marriages, which have become dull. The innumerable couples struggling with the various agonies of the man's mid-life crisis who have come to me for help during my pastorates have added to my desire to write on the problem.

DISSATISFACTION WITH MY JOB

My own mid-life crisis did not come suddenly and did not touch all areas of my life at the same time. It started with a growing unhappiness with work. When I got into the sixth year at this church, I began to feel that I was simply repeating the work of the previous five years. Nothing new was happening. I began to ask questions: "Why am I doing this? How long will I continue to do this?" Previously, the ministry had been a magnet in my life. I literally ate, drank, slept, and played with a consciousness of what I could do to make a greater spiritual impact on the lives of people and how I could cause the church I was pastoring to be more effective in its outreach for Christ.

Suddenly I began to want to escape the work. I didn't like being in the office. It often was a tedious chore to sit and counsel the troubled. I was glad to get out of extra meetings. I wanted more and more time for myself. Increasingly, I began to use the TV as a way of enabling myself not to think about my pastoral responsibilities, but the questions kept crying out for an answer. "Who am I? What do I want to do with the rest of my life? What is important?"

THE CHICKS ARE LEAVING THE NEST

When our oldest daughter Barbara went off to Taylor University, I couldn't believe that I was old enough for this to happen. We are a very tightly knit family, and now a person to whom I felt very close was leaving my life. This was the beginning of a new era that I didn't like. I cried as we left her at college, and for months afterward as I walked into her room—now strangely silent and dreadfully barren—tears welled up inside me. I felt a strong anger about living in a society that drags kids off to college, where they'll likely meet and marry someone from another part of the country. Then they'll probably take up residence a thousand miles from us so that our communications will be limited to telephone and letters. It was as if my leg had been amputated. All of my nerves said that my daughter should be here in her room, but she was gone.

Two years later the process happened again with the second daughter. You would think by now that I had accepted this change in my life, but with two-thirds of the chicks gone, the frustration only intensified. There were still so many things I wanted to do with my daughters, so many things I wanted yet to teach them, so many plans we had not carried out. Again I felt as though I were being maimed. "God, it's unfair! Life is unfair."

THE EMOTIONAL DRAIN

The church was growing very rapidly. In a four-year period the attendance climbed from 350 to more than 1,200 people. Even though the staff had increased, my workload continued to spiral. It was normal for me to work 70 to 80 hours a week, with many weeks going over 100 hours. I spent as much as 35 to 40 hours a week in private counseling with people in the church and from the community.

Each spring was getting worse. I would gradually wear down through the school year, so that by springtime I would be totally exhausted. Two years ago I collapsed in the office from physical and emotional fatigue. I found myself turning off the phone at home, not wanting to talk to people. Yet I experienced a degree of guilt because I was supposed to be serving people. Hadn't Jesus set the pattern in the Upper Room by encouraging the disciples to serve each other and not expect to be served?

MARRIAGE IGNORED

One of the problems of this kind of life is that you don't have time to work on your marriage. You are so drained by other people that you don't have the emotional capacity to give to your mate. In a sense, I was putting off the cultivating of our marriage. I was too tired to talk, to listen, to carry loads and responsibilities, and, in fact, I was too tired to even care as my wife went through a crisis period in her own life. Marriage, for me, became increasingly monotonous, but I was too preoccupied in trying to keep the church and myself going to worry about the emptiness I felt toward our marriage.

MONO STRIKES

Our two oldest daughters had each had infectious mononucleosis, and in the spring of 1977 I felt some of the same symptoms. It was a chore to drag my body around. By June I was in bed with a severe case of mono, along with some liver dysfunction. I was flat on my back day and night for two weeks. Then I was gone from the church the entire summer, resting and recuperating.

School was about to begin, and it was time for me to jump into the work full-force to prepare for the fall. But I was still physically shot and needed extra sleep. As the new semester started, I tried to keep a full schedule, but I found it increasingly difficult to help people with their troubles. I simply didn't have any emotional reserve.

By October I found that administrative decisions at the church were unbearable. People's problems caused me great anguish. I finally asked the church board for a leave of absence without pay for the month of November so I could do nothing but rest. The board asked the people of the church to pray for me and to leave me alone.

It was at this point that I decided in the middle of the night to drive south and escape from it all. I was in the grip of a full-fledged, life-shattering mid-life crisis.

Oh, for wings like a dove, to fly away and

rest! I would fly to the far off deserts and stay there. I would flee to some refuge from all this storm. (Ps. 55:6-8)

PART 2
INSIDE THE MAN

4

THE CULTURAL SQUEEZE

OUR CULTURE CAUSES A GREAT DEAL of stress on the man in mid-life. Some of this has resulted from a change in our nation's life-style. In the early part of this century 90 percent of the people lived on farms while only 10 percent lived in cities. Today that percentage has reversed. In the early 1900s people expected to live all of their life in the same community. They expected to hand their farms from one generation to another. Neighbors and friends would be lifelong companions. Today our society is extremely mobile, with more than one in every five households moving to a new location every year. Adapting to new surroundings and friends has become a way of life.

When I pastored a church in the Wheaton, Illinois, area, I visited a new family that had moved into our community. The wife apologized for the appearance of the uncut lawn, for the weeds in the flower bed, and for the bare walls inside the house. She told me that many of their boxes were not unpacked. I didn't think any of this was abnormal for a family beginning to settle in a new community, but she went on to explain that she had no intention of maintaining the yard or putting any pictures on the wall, and, in fact, one of the bedrooms would be used to store many of the items that would not be un-packed. She explained that her husband was in middle management for a growing corporation, and over the last ten years their family had moved at least once a year. It seemed a waste of time to put pictures on the wall only to take them down again in a short while. I was sadder to learn that she didn't want to get involved with the church or with any neighbors in the community, because it only caused heartache when it was time to leave.

NEW TECHNOLOGIES

Not only are we a nation on the move, but new technology and the knowledge explosion are causing a rapid job obsolescence. New industries rapidly replace old ones. New technology forces every worker into at least one job change in his life. Some predict that a young man may have to plan on at least three major job shifts in his lifetime.

Machines and computers increasingly threaten men, who view themselves as only operators. Who will they be when a machine operates their machine? "The repetitively perfect operating of the machine, assuring toler-ances and quality control far beyond those of which people are capable together with its seemingly apparent capacity to do almost anything, leaves the man who operates it or who is not yet replaced by it with a frightening sense of being replaceable."[1]

THE KNOWLEDGE EXPLOSION

Technology and knowledge have advanced together, resulting in a knowledge explosion. Knowledge didn't begin to grow rapidly until the fifteenth century with the invention of Gutenberg's movable type. From 1,000 new books a year in the sixteenth century, we have progressed to more than 1,000 new books a *week* in our time. The explosion of knowledge has caused greater specialization, but the more specialized a man is, the harder it is for him to adapt, and the more likely it is for him to become unneeded.

A WORLD ECONOMY

In the late sixties I spent three months on a trip around the world. In each country I picked up some special souvenir that couldn't be purchased in the United States—jewelry from Thailand, special wood carvings from India and the Philippines, a Greek handbag, along with other special items for each member of the family. Some of these things we proudly displayed in a china cabinet in our dining room. Now we can buy most of them at discount and drug stores. Like a modern-day Humpty Dumpty, I can't settle down comfortably on my own wall, in my own community, or even in my own nation. I'm forced to think and to compete in world terms.

Peter Drucker confirms this observation: "There has emerged a world economy in which common information generates the same economic appetites, aspirations, and demands—cutting across national boundaries and languages."[2]

CAN A MAN ADAPT?

In a rapidly changing culture, it's extremely important that we have the ability to change. One writer says that a person who has had a close relationship with his parents is more likely to be flexible and be able to change.[3] The man in his forties today may not be too adaptable, because he was raised by Depression parents. Fathers were highly oriented toward work and felt that their responsibility to their family was to provide them with a financial income, but not necessarily with an emotional income. Therefore, a man in mid-life may not be as emotionally flexible as he might have been had he been raised by parents under different circumstances.

The rapid changes of our society also contribute to a man's difficulty in adapting. Sociologists tell us there is evidence that the greatest potential for adaptability is in cultures that are not experiencing change too rapidly, especially from external events.[4] The American man in mid-life needs to be adaptable because of the rapid changes in our culture; yet these very changes are a hindrance to his flexibility.

CYNICISM

In the late sixties and early seventies the university campuses spawned great turmoil, yet offered hope. Young people believed they could change the world. Students on the university campus today have settled into a quiet cynicism that says, "You can't fight the system, but you can passively resist it."

Americans have recently become rapidly disenchanted with modern government, and cynical about its ability to perform. Politicians are frightened because they are now dealing with voters who are totally unpredictable, who don't respond to old slogans, political lines, old liberalism, or old conservatism.

The mid-life man has been hoping that everything would be figured out by this time in his life, but instead he finds himself caught in a society of cynicism and confusion.

CAUGHT BETWEEN GENERATIONS

Mid-life today is not defined by what it *is* but by what it is *between*. The man in mid-life is caught between his adolescent children and his aging parents. The parents need attention because of their age, and the children need attention because of the demands of higher education and the beginning of their careers.

The values about age are changing. The man in mid-life was brought up by parents who believed that children should respect their parents, and in most cases his parents lived to please *their* parents. The era in which we live, however, is one of the child-centered family. LeShan describes this predicament by saying, "Some-

49

times we even sold our souls for parental approval and satisfaction. . . . When we became parents, our children tended to come first; *we* worked hard at pleasing *them!* We were the first crop of parents to take our children's failures and limitations as an indication of *our* inadequacy, not theirs; the first to believe, even briefly, that one could aspire to being a perfect parent."[5]

We are a generation caught between the world that valued the aged for their wisdom and experience to teach the young, and the world now that values only youth. One of the highest compliments that can be given to a mid-life man is to say that he doesn't look his age.

Robert Raines describes this feeling of being caught in the middle:

> Middle-agers are beautiful!
> 　　aren't we, Lord?
>
> I feel for us
> 　　too radical for our parents
> 　　too reactionary for our kids
>
> 　　supposedly in the prime of life
> 　　　　like prime rib
> 　　　　everybody eating off me
> 　　　　　　devouring me
> 　　　　nobody thanking me
> 　　　　　　appreciating me
>
> 　　but still hanging in there
> 　　　　communicating with my parents
> 　　　　in touch with my kids
>
> 　　and getting more in touch
> 　　　　with myself
>
> and that's all good

thanks for making it good,

and

could you make it a little better?[6]

THE YOUTH CULT

In many cultures of the world, the young are offered sympathy for being young. The older you are, the more enthusiastically you are greeted. The Chinese, for example, equate age with wisdom. They value who you are more than what you do. In our society we tend to reverse the order. We value productivity, not the quality of life, and we are drawn more and more to worshiping youth.

The anthropologist Margaret Mead says, "I would expect to find depression among late-middle-aged men in societies where the diminutions of aging, such as the loss of strength, are important. But, if old age means having wisdom and skills that don't require physical strength, that's fine. The Australian aboriginal men, when they grow older, had all the ceremonial wisdom and so got most of the younger women, and it isn't reported to have depressed them."[7]

American men at mid-life feel frustrated because our society tells us that youth is the most valuable and desirable age and, obviously, they are no longer young. It is easy to conclude, therefore, that they are neither valuable nor desirable.

Recently I watched the television advertisements of two programs. Six of the seven ads used youth to sell their products. As one wit wrote, "Mass media continually remind the peptic generation that the 'Pepsi generation' is where it's at!"[8]

51

INSIDE THE MAN

The *Louisville Courier-Journal* published an article on mass media using youth to sell products. The article pointed out the demoralizing and humiliating message coming through that nothing good ever happens to anyone over twenty-five. The article concluded, "It isn't fair. Worse, we have a feeling that it's all too true."

John Revson, a cosmetic executive, says that the fastest growing part of his industry is the sales to men who are apparently trying to maintain youth and compete with the youth cult. "Middle-aged men today are buying 'male cosmetics' . . . 'grooming products'—because they're looking for that fountain of youth."[9]

ONLY YOUNG IS FUN

A culture that emphasizes youth puts a great deal of emotional pressure on people who are non-youth, and many are weary of having the so-called youth culture rammed down their throats. The youth cult tends to compel a man to do everything possible to stop the aging process. For a number of years now I have been jokingly telling people that I am twenty-eight years old. In my mind that is an optimum time. It is a time when a man has accumulated a little bit of experience and education and still maintains the physical vigor and energy of the twenties. The problem comes when I introduce my oldest daughter, who is now twenty-two. I won't have successfully made it through the mid-life transition until I can comfortably accept my age and let go of the fantasy of being twenty-eight.

Perhaps the greatest conflict, however, is that as youth is increasingly worshiped, the rest of life is devalued. The young then become, as someone said, "our venerable youth."[10] It comes to the point where "older people have nothing to live for, younger people nothing to grow up for."[11]

CHANGE IS ON THE WAY—PERHAPS

Ralph Barton Perry wrote in his *Plea for an Age Movement* that we should teach the world to admire wrinkles, experience, and character. Encouragingly there is some evidence on university campuses today that young people are turning toward older people and their wisdom. Older people who have something to say and who understand the young person's situation are now being sought instead of being avoided as they were during the difficult days of the sixties and early seventies. This may indicate a slight shift toward utilizing the wisdom and experience of people in the middle and later years of life.

TOO MUCH PRESSURE

People between thirty-five and fifty-five comprise about one-fourth of the population and occupy the positions of power. They make the decisions, but they also pay the bills and carry the major responsibility for the other three-fourths of the population.

Meanwhile, pressures come from the community. Magazine articles, doctors, and wives nag the man in mid-life to slow down and relax, but he finds his telephone ringing all the time. He is asked to support this cause, be on that board, be involved in this fund raising campaign. A leader is needed for the youth group, someone with his travel experience is wanted to speak at school, and on and on and on.

As the pressures mounted on me this past fall, my congregation knew from my comments or from explanations by the Board of Leadership that I was under a great deal of stress. People were asked to divert their requests for help or additional ministries to other members of the staff. After one of these announcements in the morning service, two university students came to me and asked if there was a time during the week when the three of us could meet together so they could pray that God would enable me to have more time to relax. I tried to be as kind as possible as I suggested to them that they pray in their own rooms and allow me to have that time to myself.

It's easy for a man in mid-life to be conditioned to follow the expectations of other people. In the past, if you wanted to succeed, you did what your boss suggested; if you wanted to be respected in the community, you served on various committees; if you wanted to be considered spiritual, you got involved in every program of the church. The problem is that this pattern, if not thoughtfully analyzed, means living a life directed by others rather than one's own choices based on the unique creation God has made us to be.

FAMILY PRESSURES

Family responsibilities also put pressure on a man in mid-life. In these years he must maintain a home large enough for the children and all of their activities. At the same time, he must provide money for a college education and the launching of the children into their own careers. And he may have financial responsibilities for aging parents at the same time he is supposed to be preparing for his own retirement.

Sally and I were married in June, 1954, and that fall we started seminary in Denver. All of our possessions fit into a small four-by-four trailer as we pulled into the Mile-High City. Fifteen years later, when we made our last move, it required two sixteen-foot U-Haul trucks, and we had sold some of our possessions before loading. Today we would need two twenty-foot trucks, each pulling a fourteen-foot trailer! I sometimes wonder how in the world we got all this "junk" and think what a terrible waste of funds it is to keep it.

I often wonder if there will ever be enough money. This church, though not wealthy, is generous to us. Each month I watch hundreds of dollars melt away like butter on a hot griddle. I wonder where it has all gone. There never seems to be anything left over to prepare for the future or even to do those nice little things together as a couple.

WORK PRESSURE

Work is also applying pressure to the man in mid-life. Let's not delude ourselves; we're not as fast as we used to be. When I play racquetball, my mind says, "Reach! Stretch! Get that ball!" My body says to my mind, "Who are you kidding?" There is no question that I cannot stand the long work hours I used to be able to take. My body doesn't spring back as quickly when I'm up late at night counseling someone or attending a meeting.

In a recent visit to my doctor, he again urged me to slow down. I told him the problem is that I know what it takes to make a church go. It takes a great deal of energy, creativity, training, and just plain hours of work. To cut back on my time from eighty hours a week to forty would mean that ministries in the church would suffer, people would not be visited, departments or programs in the church that are floundering would not get the additional leadership help they need. All of these would affect the church and, ultimately, how people would view me in my effectiveness as a pastor. The truth is, we live in a competitive world. If I can't cut it, there are dozens of younger men who can. The same is true of any profession, business, or job.

There is a concept in business called the Peter Principle; that is, a man will be advanced in his work and be given greater and greater responsibility until he literally becomes incompetent. Most businesses then release the man rather than move him back to the level of his competence.

The man in mid-life may follow a pattern for ten to fifteen years of striving for success and continually extending himself. His body and mind have been able to carry that pressure up to now. In mid-life two forces may converge in his work life. He may have been pushed to a level of responsibility that is beyond him, thus causing frustration, and his body is probably slowing down and unable to stand the stress. His job, therefore, may become increasingly dissatisfying.

JUST A MACHINE

One result of all this pressure is extreme frustration. He may find himself living by other peoples' goals and feel angry at them as well as at himself for allowing this to happen. But he cannot change now. He is too deeply committed to a direction. He may feel that everyone is taking from his life.

I said to Sally at one point, "I feel like a vending machine, dispensing products. Someone pushes a button, and out comes a sermon. Someone pushes another button for a solution to a personal or administrative problem. The family pushes buttons, and out come dollars or time involvement. The community pushes other buttons, and I show up at meetings, sign petitions, and take stands." It's easy for a man in mid-life to feel that he is trapped with obligations to everyone, and the frustration is that he can't get out. In my twenties, however, these demands were all handled with enthusiasm.

The second result of the pressure of work may be a feeling of inadequacy. A man's body is slowing down, and if he compares himself to some of the Young Turks coming up in the organization, his inadequacy may be intensified. When he begins to look around at the job market, he realizes that there is a great deal of age discrimination. The number of jobs available to him that produce the money he needs for this time in life are shriveling. A pastor friend said to me recently, "You know, I'm really fortunate to have been called to this church, because I'm now over fifty." The mid-life man may also feel inadequate because of the knowledge explosion, and younger men may seem to have brighter, newer ideas.

The third result of the pressures of work is fatigue. Our man is tired of trying to keep up with the demands of the community; he's had it with the increasing pressure at work; he's simply tired of having a tired body. Alvin Toffler describes some of this desperate fatigue in *Future Shock*. The man in mid-life doesn't have time to pursue art or music. He doesn't have time for contemplation, watching things grow, looking at a sunset. He's like a hamster, running on the little wheel in his cage—he has to keep running to keep his balance. Scarf quotes a man who is struggling with the pressures of life and who accurately expresses the fatigue that many men feel: "I feel a weakening of the need to be a great man and an increasing feeling of let's just get through this the best way we can. Never mind hitting any home runs. Let's just get through the ballgame without getting beaned."[12]

> But I am a worm, not a man, scorned and despised by my own people and by all mankind. Everyone who sees me mocks and sneers and shrugs. . . . "Is this the one who claims the Lord delights in him? We'll believe it when we see God rescue him!" (Ps. 22:6-8)

5
SECOND ADOLESCENCE

THE TEENAGE BOY IS MOVING from childhood into that long era of success-oriented and active young adult life. The man at mid-life is moving from that active, aggressive period of young adulthood to the long plateau of the middle years.

Like the teenager, the man in the mid-life crisis has three basic areas that cause him difficulty.

THE MID-LIFE MAN'S BODY

First, they both are trying to handle the physical changes of their bodies. The teenager is rapidly growing taller and filling out his body to that of a man. He has trouble with the spiraling increase in his sexual drive, and he is embarrassed by acne and his changing voice.

The man in his forties is also having physical problems. His weight is beginning to shift toward the trunk of his body. His muscles no longer have the tone they once had. His skin is beginning to sag. He is losing that beautiful hair. He runs out for a pass in a game of backyard football with his son and almost drops from exhaustion. There is probably a *de*crease in his sexual capacity. And, insult of insults, he may also have some acne problems.

THE MID-LIFE MAN'S FEELINGS

The second area of problems is psychological. Sometimes the adolescent has expanding aggressive energies. His moods swing from great joy to restlessness to depression to gloom. The teenager is also known for his grumbling. He complains about school, his parents, his youth group; in fact, very few things in life really satisfy him. The teenager has some problem putting things into perspective. He can't really get a grasp on the childhood from which he came, and he has trouble clearly seeing the future. He is extremely introspective; he sits with his headphones on listening to a record, totally lost in another world by himself.

The man in the mid-life crisis wrestles with astoundingly similar problems. His son, for example, may be asking, "What is sex all about?" The father is asking, "How soon will I lose it?" He may be worried because it takes him longer to achieve an erection before intercourse. His physical and emotional fatigue may cause him to feel he is becoming impotent, and sex may occupy much of his thought.

The mid-life man also is wrestling with aggressive feelings toward the young men who are coming up beneath him to replace him at work. He has aggressive feelings toward society, family, and even God for putting so much pressure on him and for making life what it is.

Similar to the teenager, the man has giant mood swings. At one point things are going along quite well; the next thing you know, he is in his car, driving off somewhere to be alone. There may be times of great productivity and at other times lethargy.

The teenager grumbles about everything in life, and the man in mid-life grumbles about his children, his wife, his job, work around the house, taxes, politics, every duty and responsibility. All of life seems to be sour.

In the same way as his teenager, this man has lost perspective. He thinks that the crisis he is experiencing is the sum total of his life. He can't see it as a developmental process from his earlier, young-adult life. He cannot seem to accept the plateau that is ahead of him. Lost in his present crisis, he becomes adolescent in his introspection, totally absorbed within himself, and sometimes almost oblivious to the world around him as he stares into space.

THE MID-LIFE MAN'S FRIENDS

A third area of trouble for both the teenager and the man at mid-life is social relationships. One day parents believe that there is a deep relationship between their teenager and another friend, and the next day the two are not speaking to each other. The man at mid-life also has problems socially. For a while his friends really take it on the chin. Sometimes he is very rude, with no time for people. He declares, "I want to be with the people I want to be with, when I want to be with them." He is quite often disenchanted with the world around him. He may have been involved intensively in big business, but now may be disgusted with the selfish, dollar-oriented direction of his company and not be shy in telling them so. There are times when he enjoys being with his wife; there are other times when he simply wants to escape everything and everybody. In short, he may become very antisocial.

IDENTITY CRISIS

Both the teenager and the man at mid-life are having an identity crisis. Each is asking: "Who am I? What are my values? What do I want to do with my life?" The difference, however, is that the boy is asking the questions looking to the future; the father is asking the questions looking back at the past as well as toward the future. Fried says of this crisis, "Where forty and four-teen differ, of course, is that this is the second time around for the adult: what he is involved in is not so much a quest for identity as an inquest."[1]

Sometimes the teenager is quite angry at the environment that has made him the way he is; that is, his world, his parents, and God. The man in his forties cannot totally blame the environment for who he is now, and deep within himself he realizes that he is the result of the choices he has made. In some ways, this intensifies his anger.

One dentist expressed the unhappiness he felt this way: "Sure, I feel trapped. Why shouldn't I? Twenty-five years ago a dopey eighteen-year-old college kid made up *his mind* that *I* was going to be a dentist. So now here I am, a dentist. I'm stuck. What I want to know is, who told that kid he could decide what I was going to have to do for the rest of my life?"[2]

THE CRISIS IS NECESSARY

We all know that adolescence is an important part of development. This is the time when the teenager will try out new attitudes, behaviors, ways of thinking, and establish a philosophy of life. Parents have learned that it is important to encourage this process and to stand alongside to provide the necessary support so that the young person can successfully navigate these difficult waters.

The man in his forties also needs to be encouraged to face similar issues. People need to stand alongside in support and encourage the man not to run from the process but rather to let the developmental process mature him for the next stage in life.

The adolescent and the man in mid-life will change as they pass through their respective crises. They will not be entirely the same men they were before, for these are the two key times in life when the clay will be "thrown" repeatedly on the potter's wheel and the pot formed again and again until it is exactly the desired expression of the potter.

Each of them will relinquish some of the old patterns of life, some of the old ways of viewing themselves and the world. The Bible says, "When I was a child I spoke and thought and reasoned as a child does. But when I became a man my thoughts grew far beyond those of my childhood, and now I have put away the childish things" (I Cor. 13:11).

The man has at least one advantage over his son. He can now evaluate all of his life and set new directions from a broad base of skills, status, power, and experience that his son does not have.

There is, however, one danger the man at mid-life faces that the adolescent doesn't. The man in his forties is going through this complex developmental change in the context of day-to-day responsibilities. His teenage son can plop on the headphones and step into another world without hurting other people. The man in mid-life has the responsibilities of caring for a family, maintaining his productivity at work, paying the bills, repairing the appliances, continuing the community contacts; in short, it is almost impossible for him simply to run away. He must deal with real life around him while struggling with the conflicts inside.

> I keep thinking of the good old days of the past, long since ended. Then my nights were filled with joyous songs. I search my soul and meditate upon the difference now.

> I think of God and moan, overwhelmed with longing for his help. I cannot sleep until you act. I am too distressed even to pray! (Ps. 77: 5-6, 3-4)

6
THE ENEMY HORDE

THE MAN IN MID-LIFE has now identified four major enemies in his life.

ENEMY #1

The first foe is his body. It is aging, slowing down, and losing youthful appeal. When he was younger and women looked admiringly at him, it gave him a sense of pride, but now they don't even look anymore. If only he could do something about his body to change it in some way!

He is aggravated that he does not have the energy and stamina of his earlier days. He has trouble accepting the fact that his muscles are getting flabby and it is easier to gain weight.

ENEMY #2

The second enemy is his work. How in the world did he ever get trapped into this job? Why would anyone in his right mind want to be president of Amalgamated Chemical? What is this going to mean in the long run of life anyway? Yes, he wants to be famous, but not for this. He wants to do something significant for the world, to bring peace and happiness and hope to people.

Or it may be that he has not made it to the presidency, and he sees now that he is never going to. He is on a treadmill, grinding through the boring daily routine in order to meet his heavy financial obligations. Instead of an enjoyable challenge, work has become oppressive.

ENEMY #3

The third enemy is his wife and family. You see, if it weren't for his massive domestic responsibilities, he'd give up his job immediately. He's hated it for years anyway, but it provides the $70,000 a year he needs for his house, three cars, and cottage on the lake, not to mention keeping the kids in college and taking vacations to various parts of the world. If he didn't have all of these family responsibilities, he could give up his job and do something more simple. He could live off the land. If he weren't married, he could knock around like some young people are doing. He could simply get on a motorcycle with a couple of sleeping bags, a tent, and a young woman and start roaming the country.

THE ULTIMATE ENEMY

The fourth enemy is God. The mid-life man pictures God leaning over the banister of Heaven, grinning fiendishly and pointing a long, bony finger as he says, "You despicable, disgraceful Christian! You are the worst possible example of a mature man. You are selfish. You are filled with lust. You are lazy. You are so disgusting that I want to spew you out of my mouth!"

The man in mid-life views God not only as an enemy but as an *unfair* enemy. He says to God, "You made me this way. You gave me these drives and interests. You knew all about the change that would be coming in my life. You are the one who allowed the human body to age and finally die. You are the one who is really, ultimately, to blame for the mess I'm in now!"

This blaming of God is much the same as the animosity Adam expressed to God in the Garden of Eden. After Adam and Eve had disobeyed God, God came to talk with them, as his habit had been, and said, "Adam, where are you?"

Adam responded, "I'm over here, hiding behind this tree."

"Why are you hiding, Adam?"

And Adam replied, "Well, you see, God, I'm naked."

So God asked, "Who told you that you were naked? Have you eaten fruit from the tree I warned you about?"

Adam, realizing then that he was exposed, began to shift the blame. "The woman—it was that woman *you* gave me! It was not only her fault, God, but actually it was *your* fault too, for you were the one involved in creation. You knew that this was going to happen; therefore, it's your fault."

So, also, the man in mid-life crisis identifies God as his unfair enemy.

> Who will protect me from the wicked? Who will be my shield? I would have died unless the Lord had helped me. I screamed, "I'm slipping, Lord!" and he was kind and saved me.
>
> Lord, when doubts fill my mind, when my heart is in turmoil, quiet me and give me renewed hope and cheer. (Ps. 94:16-19)

PART 3

DEAD-END ROADS

7
DEPRESSION

THE MAN IN THE MID-LIFE CRISIS will try many different solutions to reduce the tension in his life and to escape from his enemies. Most of the methods he'll try in the early days of the crisis are escape-oriented, which, in fact, are not real solutions and many times will compound the problem.

He's like a little boy lost in a crowd of people at a shopping center. He goes one direction, thinking that he sees some legs that look familiar to him, only to find that they are not those of his parents. He turns another direction, but again he finds it doesn't lead him to his parents, and he is more lost than ever.

Because the mid-life man thinks other people are causing his problems, he uses tactics to eliminate those enemies from his life. He will probably try several dead-end roads before he begins to realize that the causes of the crisis are primarily internal, not external. Perhaps he will have to be frustrated by working through several of his escape solutions before he can look at himself and life in reality.

FEELING DOWN

One of the most common responses of the man struggling with the mid-life crisis is to drop into depression. It's the easiest escape and the one that comes most naturally. It is the logical progression of all the events we've looked at in the previous chapters. Depression is the natural outcome of the conflict of forces pressing upon his life and the explosive anger, frustration, bitterness, and self-pity building within him.

At work he sits and stares at his papers, or he idly watches his machine work. He seems only to do his job if he is prodded by someone else. He isn't thinking about anything in particular; he just feels crummy and depressed. His productivity drops off. If he works in a creative/think business, he loses the capacity for creativity. He is short-tempered with everyone. People who work under him say he is very difficult to please and is always finding small things wrong with the way they are doing the job.

At home he seems to have dropped out as well. If he was a handyman, he doesn't do the little things around the house and yard he used to do. Sometimes he simply sits in a chair and gazes out the window or listens endlessly to music or stares at television. He avoids conversation. He dodges leadership and problem-solving. His temper flares up, and he says to his wife and children, "I just want to be left alone! Can't you understand that?"

Of course his marriage suffers. He talks only about surface topics. As for sex, well, it's usually, "Not tonight, dear, I'm too tired."

Depression spills over into social relationships, and he withdraws from late-night coffees, card games, bowling, or dinner with friends from church. He explains to his wife that he doesn't want to be around people. Repeatedly, he is off on long walks, rides on the bike, or drives in the car.

Many such men, when interviewed and asked to describe their feelings about work, marriage, and life in general, say they are bored. They feel life is a farce, a dumb thing they're continuing to do. The word *bore* means "to make something empty," and this is what has happened in the job, the marriage, and all of life.

EARLY CHALLENGES

When the man was in his twenties, he had goals, things to accomplish, mountains to climb. There were exciting new things to learn, skills to master, and relationships to develop.

In my twenties I set out some goals for my life. I didn't sit down one day and write a complete list of priorities, but I found, as I went through college and came to understand myself and God better, that certain targets began to crystallize in my mind. I wanted to succeed in college and to overcome the educational inadequacy of my earlier years, and I wanted to become more acceptable to other people socially. I had a goal of finding the right wife and raising a warm family who would love each other and God. I wanted to ably explain the Scriptures and God to people and to be an effective counselor. I had another goal of becoming a good public speaker and being able to move people with words. I wanted to pastor a large church (in my thinking then, a church over 1,000 was large). I wanted to travel around the world. I even had goals of being on radio and television and writing books and magazine articles. I felt that many of these goals would provide a lifetime of challenge.

OUT OF CHALLENGES

All of the goals I envisioned in my early twenties have been fulfilled, except one. I still have a goal of being the president of a college or seminary some day. (Some of my friends who know of this goal of mine assure me that it's one of the worst jobs in the world!) However, one of the causes for my depression and boredom was that I had run out of goals. For me to successfully come through this mid-life crisis in my life, I needed to reestablish some of the old goals and allow God to lead me into new goals for this long and, hopefully, productive mid-life plateau.

MID-LIFE MAN IN THE PSALMS

The man in the mid-life crisis who sinks into depression identifies very closely with the writer of Psalm 102. Whoever wrote it was certainly familiar with anxiety and was able to spell out in brief form some of the causes of his own personal depression.

Shortness of life is one cause of his depression. "For my days disappear like smoke. . . . My life is passing swiftly as the evening shadows. I am withering like grass. . . . He has cut me down in middle life, shortening my days" (vv. 3, 11, 23). It seems that all of us try to resist the process of aging and death.

Poor health is another problem. "My health is broken" (v. 3). In the mid-years the physical health becomes an increasing problem. These are the years of the heart attack, the time when diabetes increases and when a tumor of the prostate may be discovered. In short, the body is beginning to show some toll physically.

The writer of Psalm 102 says that he is *emotionally unable to cope*, and this also produces depression. He says, "My heart is sick" (v. 4), and he uses the illustration of grass that is trampled and withered. This is a pre-ulcer state of mind. He is unable to handle the problems of life, and the unresolved problems increase his inability to handle problems. In other words, emotional stress is cyclical. It is like a giant whirlpool, sucking ever to the center and increasing in intensity.

The Psalmist also says that *loss of appetite* depresses him, yet, at the same time his depression produces a loss of appetite. "My food is tasteless, I have lost my appetite" (v. 4). Literally, food becomes unimportant. The King James Version says, "I forget to eat my bread." The writer is preoccupied with his problems and, thus, loses his appetite. Weight loss is very common during times of great anxiety. The result of the loss of appetite is that "I am reduced to skin and bones" (v. 5). The loss of nourishment compounds the problem and tends to increase anxiety and depression.

Loneliness is another reason for his depression. "I am like a vulture in a far-off wilderness, or like an owl alone in the desert. I lie awake, lonely as a solitary sparrow on the roof" (vv. 6-7). Each of the birds describes a special kind of loneliness. The vulture represents the loneliness experienced at the end of life—death. The owl is pictured alone, hooting from an isolated branch by himself at night. The sparrow is not thought of as a lonely bird, but the Psalmist carefully sets apart this bird as a "solitary sparrow" alone on the roof. Sparrows are ordinarily in groups, but this one sits awake by himself on the roof.

The Psalmist also says that he is depressed because he is *mocked by his enemies:* "My enemies taunt me day after day and curse at me" (v. 8). Success brings with it not only a feeling of having arrived but also an unmentioned fear that other people are waiting for you to fall. The higher you move up the ladder of success and achievement, the smaller the number of people ahead of you, and the greater the number of people beneath you who are looking for opportunities to peck you to death.

The Psalmist writes that humiliation, or *loss of poise,* control, and stability, is another reason for his depression. Here is a man who is sitting, weeping, in utter mourning and humiliation. As he lifts a cup of water to his lips, his tears drop into the cup. He is a broken man with a life out of control.

Next, the Psalmist lists the problem of *not being recognized* by the world. His life is coming to an end. He has lived this long and done nothing of significance. "My life is passing swiftly as the evening shadows. I am withering like grass, while you, Lord, are a famous King forever. Your fame will endure to every generation" (vv. 11-12). The Psalmist paints a contrasting picture: I am a passing, finite, frail, dying human who has accomplished nothing, but *you,* God, are secure, famous, and everyone from generation to generation will continue to remember you. He has a short, limited life that will die off, while God is well known to the world and continues to outlive one generation after another.

Impending death is another source of his depression:

"He has cut me down in middle life, shortening my days" (v. 23). A young man sees life as endless. Even though he knows that death will come some day, it will always come to someone else. But the man in mid-life sees death as an imminent reality. He realizes his days are numbered, and each time the sun rises or sets, another segment of his life has been cut off.

The human personality tends naturally to reach out for solutions to depression and anxiety. The difficulty is that the solutions he is trying are not effective, and many of the problems he is facing do not have human solutions. There is no way that the Psalmist can lengthen his life, avoid death, or on his own strength become famous, or change the mind of an enemy, or eliminate a physical health problem.

WILL ALCOHOL ANSWER?

The problem with depression is that it is essentially a vacuum and not an answer. Our lives won't tolerate a vacuum, and sooner or later something will rush in to fill that emptiness. All too often, it is alcohol. Alcoholism is one of the country's major health problems, affecting more than 80 million people, if we include both alcoholics and those who live and work with them. It's not only a nationwide problem, but it is a major problem for people in mid-life. Alcoholism increases 50 percent among people in the forty-to-sixty age bracket compared to those in their thirties.

Alcoholism is a self-defeating process that affects a man's output at work, his relationships at home, and his contacts with other people. He feels he is escaping from his problem but, in fact, it is intensified. Just beneath the surface of our personalities lies a great deal of immaturity, anger, and resentment that has been carefully kept in check, but alcohol releases these inhibitions. Remarks expressed at work, home, or social gatherings when he is under the influence of alcohol drive away the very people who could be the most help to him.

DRINKING DEPLETES HIM

Because the man at mid-life is struggling with questions of his sexual prowess, he sometimes feels that alcohol will free him up and enable him to express himself more adequately sexually. The truth is just the opposite. Alcohol tends to diminish potency and make the man less effective in carrying out intercourse.

Alcohol also works against him physically. He is already feeling tired and run-down and, in fact, he may need to be on a different kind of diet to build his body. Alcohol adds to his physical depletion.

The man in mid-life who hides behind alcohol is also emotionally miserable. According to one expert, he has a "low self-esteem, self-pity, a tendency toward self-punishment, resentment, an inclination to project blame for trouble elsewhere, excessive impatience, irritability, tension, depression, stubbornness, anxiety, jealousy . . . the list is almost endless. But all these characteristics can be condensed into three major ones: egocentricity, a low tolerance for tension, and hidden feelings of dependency offset by conscious feelings of omnipotence."[1]

Alcohol is not really an answer. It just exaggerates the problems, isolates a man from people, intensifies his feeling of guilt, and works hand-in-hand with depression. Hiding in alcohol may be like getting into quicksand, which sucks a man down deeper and deeper into the mid-life crisis and takes him further away from people, God, and real solutions.

GOD IS A FRIEND

We can find real help for depression by involving God and laying the causes for depression at his feet. To begin with, as the Psalmist indicates, God is concerned. "He will listen to the prayers of the destitute, for he is never too busy to heed their requests" (v. 17). God knows we are poor and in need, and he loves us. The Bible says that Jesus was tempted in all ways like we are and understands us: "But Jesus the Son of God is our great High Priest who has gone to heaven itself to help us; therefore let us never stop trusting him. This High Priest of ours understands our weaknesses, since he had the same temptations we do, though he never once gave way to them and sinned. So let us come boldly to the very throne of God and stay there to receive his mercy and to find grace to help us in our times of need" (Heb. 4:14-16).

The writer of Psalm 102 bares his heart in the struggle with depression, but he also points us to God who understands. It seems to be no mistake in the planning of God that the words of Psalm 102, showing the anguish of a man at mid-life, are placed next to the comfort and encouragement of Psalm 103, which shows the heart-concern of God as people struggle with problems.

He forgives all my sins. He heals me. He ransoms me from hell. He surrounds me with lovingkindness and tender mercies. He fills my life with good things! My youth is renewed like the eagle's! . . .

He is merciful and tender toward those who don't deserve it; he is slow to get angry and full of kindness and love. He never bears a grudge, nor remains angry forever. He has not punished us as we deserve for all our sins, for his mercy toward those who fear and honor him is as great as the height of the heavens above the earth. He has removed our sins as far away from us as the east is from the west. He is like a father to us, tender and sympathetic to those who reverence him. For he knows we are but dust, and that our days are few and brief, like grass, like flowers, blown by the wind and gone forever. (vv. 3-5, 8-15)

The answer is in allowing God to define whom we should be; what we should be doing with our lives, days, and hours; and what our goals and aspirations ought to be for the future.

HOPE AND HELP

Roger Barrett, professor of psychology at Malone College, has written an extremely helpful book entitled *Depression—What It Is and What to Do About It,* in which he says, "Depression is beginning to rival schizophrenia as the nation's number one mental health problem. . . . One out of every ten persons in the U. S. may become clinically depressed at some point in their lives."[2]

Dr. Barrett, in a very practical and down-to-earth manner, talks about depression—how it starts; some of the childhood contributions and developments; how anger, inferiority, and guilt are involved in depression. He also helps Christians understand the difference between real and false guilt. He shows the disastrous effect that living under the Law can have in producing depression in a Christian's life. He gives sane and helpful suggestions for people who are wrestling with depression. Most importantly he indicates that there is hope and help for the man in mid-life in the throes of depression.

I waited patiently for God to help me; then he listened and heard my cry. He lifted me out of the pit of despair, out from the bog and the mire, and set my feet on a hard, firm path and steadied me as I walked along. He has given me a new song to sing, of praises to our God. (Ps. 40:1-3)

8
A NEW SHELL

The time for wild kisses goes fast and it's
Time for Sanka
Already?

Judith Viorst

ABOUT A YEAR AGO I saw a picture of some people from my era who had gathered for a college reunion. What a shock! These people had lost their hair and their shapes. The women looked frazzled and frowsy. The men who had been athletic and really big with the college girls looked tired, conservative, and just plain old. I thought, *Wow! I'm glad I'm not like those old people,* and then I had a second thought: *I'm glad I wasn't there to have my picture taken.*

A NEW BODY

To put it very bluntly, the man's body in mid-life is beginning to show visible signs of crumbling. Like an ancient building, the roof is in trouble, mortar is coming out of the joints, the floors are sagging, and the doors creak. However, there is a large conspiracy today that continually tells us that outward appearance and productivity are the only things that count.

People whom you thought were your friends are suddenly your enemies. When you casually ask your dentist about a problem with a tooth, he says, "Well, for a man of your age . . ." You suggest to the barber that perhaps he could comb your hair to cover the bald spot, and he says, "When you hit forty, you have to expect some of these things."

Biologically speaking, aging occupies about three-quarters of our life. The fastest growth takes place in the life of the unborn child. Growth is rapid in the infant and the young child, but is progressively slower until about age twenty-one, when it peaks. Growth now begins to change toward decline. The man in his twenties and thirties is not much aware of it. He notices he *is* slowing down a bit, but he jokingly passes it off.

When he hits forty, however, he begins to identify his body as an enemy that is making him look old. He frantically attempts to change his appearance to win the battle with age and stay perpetually young. Gloria Heidi in her book, *Winning the Age Game*, says, "And what comes first in winning the age game? Updating your physical appearance comes first. . . . When you look *great* and know it, you feel great and show it; and somehow when your morale zooms, other, more serious problems become manageable."[1] So a man believes that if he can only change his body, get the muscle tone back, and reduce the flab, he's going to solve his mid-life crisis.

His attempt to create a new body is not all negative. If he can get his body into better shape, it will improve his self-image, his confidence among people, and also help some of his problems with stamina.

BEAUTY IS GOOD

Joyce Brothers, well-known and popular psychologist, points out in *Better than Ever* that "beautiful people have beautiful personalities. . . . We consistently judge them to be more sensitive, kind, intelligent, interesting, sociable, and exciting than less attractive people."[2]

Dr. Brothers goes on to speak of a study made in a school among kindergartners and teachers regarding the people to whom they were most often attracted: "They [the children] picked the most attractive children as their favorites. Their teachers did likewise, and considered the less attractive children more likely to be troublemakers."[3] She continues, "When we grow up, for both men and women, higher salary levels and greater advancement have a high correlation with pleasant looks, at all ages and in all fields."[4]

FAT IS BAD

The New York Times reported an interesting study by Robert Half, the president of a chain of employment agencies. He evaluated the salaries of 15,000 agency executives. "Of 1,500 executives who earned between $25,000 and $45,000 a year, only 9 percent were more than ten pounds overweight, while of the 13,500 executives who earned between $10,000 and $20,000, almost 40 percent were more than 10 percent—a bit more than ten pounds—overweight."[5] Mr. Half commented that his offices received thousands of requests for thin people but the only request they had ever had for a fat one came from a company that made clothing for overweight men.

A man might erroneously believe that by getting his body back into shape, he is going to erase the years and suddenly regain his youth. The truth is that he is not going to become young again; however, the side benefits of an improved body are extremely great. As he gets his body in shape, he will be less likely to experience ailments such as heart attack. Greater physical activity will tend to decrease depression, and he will be able to handle greater pressure. He will feel better about himself as he takes off pounds.

A NEW WARDROBE

It is true that our society is contriving to make youth *be* and *last* the total life. So a man not only fights to make his body look younger, but also to make the packaging look younger. The way we look does have a direct bearing upon the way we feel about ourselves. We can't erase age, but in the process of wearing current styles we may feel better about ourselves. Wearing up-to-date clothing also helps the world to view us as people who understand the present age and are worth hearing. So, though the initial motivation may be wrong, the outcome will have positive contributions in helping a man through the mid-life crisis.

GRAY HAIR ON THAT MANLY CHEST

There is a definite difference between trying to dress fashionably in current styles and trying to appear like a twenty-year-old swinger who just came off the beach. There is nothing quite so comical as a fifty-year-old man in too-tight hip huggers with carefully dyed but thin hair combed down over his forehead, a shirt unbuttoned to his waist, and a cross hanging on the gray hair of his chest.

Joel and Lois Davitz quote a young clothing salesman in a men's wear store regarding the tastes of the middle-aged customers. "I've seen it a thousand times. They start swinging when they're pushing up near fifty. Want style. They come in here wearing conservative cuts, dark gray and blue, and they walk out with vents, plaids, gold buttons, hot pink shirts. I had one guy in here this morning—looked like a VP: was in a gray flannel suit, white shirt, cuff links. You'll never believe me when I tell you he walks out of here in a turtleneck, bell trousers, a jacket I couldn't unload on a teenager at half the price. You should have seen the plaid. He asks me how does he look. You make a two hundred buck sale; the guy is standing there with a paunch, gray hair, bags under his eyes, and what do you say? You tell me."[6]

A NEW LIFE-STYLE

So our man has trimmed down his weight, has his muscles back into shape, and is wearing a very different style of clothing. All of these are a part of his changing life-style. He seems ready now to do what he wants to do and to try to be more himself. He may spend less time at his work and more time in leisure activities. Completely new hobbies and pastimes might become important to him. He may trade his conservative family-style car for a sports model.

This attempt at a new life-style may cause people around him to say that he's entering his second childhood. He's trying to live a life-style that, in some ways, is catch-up—doing some of the things he didn't get to do in his teens and twenties. Now there is a great urgency to carry out those activities.

A pastor friend of mine who was extremely successful, pastoring a large church with a multistaff, decided he had had it. The church seemed to be moving so slowly, and no one really wanted to do anything creative or aggressive. He was tired of the lethargy of boards and committees, so he decided to drop out. He resigned the church, moved to another part of the country, and went back to school. He also felt he needed some time to be away from his family, so he bought a large motorcycle and all of the necessary gear and set off across the country at his own pace, stopping wherever he wanted for as long as he wanted, doing his own thing. He traveled about three-quarters of the way across the United States before he returned to his family and his studies.

The Frenchman Paul Gauguin is an example of a man who changed directions in mid-life. Gauguin worked for a stockbrokerage firm in Paris from 1871 to 1883 and was also an amateur painter. He kept dreaming of how wonderful it would be to live in peace in Tahiti, to spend his time painting and be free from the struggle for money. After several years of dreaming, Gauguin did move to Tahiti and became one of the world's famous artists.

COLLEGE FRIENDS

When I was in college, three fellows and I had an especially close friendship. Each of us sensed that God had called us into the ministry. We talked and prayed and were involved in some ministries together. We hitchhiked together, shared our meager financial resources, helped each other with studies, and shared the joys and sadnesses of each other's love lives. When college was over, we separated, three of us going to seminaries and eventually into local churches. The fourth man pastored a church upon graduation and then became a Youth for Christ director.

Now we all are at mid-life, and we learn, as we get in touch with each other over the distances, that three of the four of us are going through crisis times. The fourth man does not seem to be experiencing the same crisis. It appears that the death of his wife when he was in his early thirties accelerated the whole process of crisis for him. He married a second wife who is more than ten years younger than he, and he is not now going through what the other three of us are experiencing.

All three of us have been involved in a succession of successful pastorates, but in the last couple of years each has grown restless. One man left a long pastorate and moved to a new church. There he was unwilling to put up with the politicking and intrachurch conflicts. He abruptly resigned, moved to the West Coast, and started doctoral studies. He and his wife are presently involved in counseling married couples. Their life-style has been sharply altered. They seem more relaxed and less pressured by the expectations of people.

The second man pastored churches where his salary was always less than adequate, even though the churches were relatively large. His wife had to work most of the time. He had very successful ministries in a number of churches, earning recognition from church leaders and from business and community people. He began to feel a growing urgency to, somehow, sometime in his life, enjoy a few of the material pleasures and financial benefits that some of his business friends were enjoying. Was it really fair that he should be serving God, ministering unselfishly to people, while his family lived near poverty and he could make almost no preparation for retirement? This growing dissatisfaction led him out of the ministry and into business.

SAILBOAT OR MOTORCYCLE?

I am the third of the trio, and my life-style also has begun to change. Previously, I had no time for recreation or days off, because there was a world to be reached and an endless stream of people to be helped. A little over a year ago, however, I began to have the urge to do something to get away occasionally. Our family bought a sixteen-foot catamaran, and I began to sail. My work became only one of many things I did, rather than the only thing.

During a flight layover in a large city, I called one of my seminary friends to see how he was doing. As we talked, I shared with him that I was in the process of writing a book on men at mid-life. He laughed loudly over the phone. "You can use me as a prime example of a change in life-style," he said. I was surprised, because he was always fastidiously dressed, careful about how people saw him, and extremely well controlled. He revealed to me that he now owned a motorcycle and was riding back and forth to church on it. He felt comfortable wearing jeans and cut-offs to the church office. In general, he was following a rather hang-loose style of living.

Since our conversation, he has resigned his church, which he had built essentially from scratch into a very large, thriving organism. He was ready for a different kind of ministry and has accepted a teaching position at a graduate school. Even though his salary is reduced, the benefits of a new challenge far outweigh the lessened income.

OVER THE OCEAN BLUE

The story of a life-style change that grabs me most is the story of Robert Manry, recorded in his book, *Tinkerbelle*. The story is close to me, because Manry lived in Cleveland, Ohio. I was raised in Cleveland, and as a boy I delivered the *Cleveland Plain Dealer*. Robert Manry worked for the *Plain Dealer* as an unimportant copyeditor. At forty-seven, Manry decided he had to do some things with his life that were fun. He never dreamed, though, that they would lead to a change in his total life-style.

Manry was a little nuts about sailing, and that's the second reason I'm attracted to his story. Sailors are essentially dreamers, and it's easy for me to identify with his dreams to sail across the Atlantic Ocean. A friend of his who owned a twenty-five-foot boat asked Manry if he would sail with him across the ocean. Manry leaped at the opportunity and began to plan for all that was involved in making the trip. Shortly before they were to set out on the voyage, Manry's friend backed out. Manry's dreams were on the verge of being shattered. He then began to secretly make plans for the trip alone in *Tinker-*

belle, his own 13½-foot boat. For the next several months he carried out his preparations and secretly equipped his boat for the trip. Only his wife and a few close friends knew he was going to try to cross the Atlantic in this small boat.

On June 1, 1965, Manry, in his little white boat with the red sail, left Falmouth, Massachusetts, bound for Falmouth, England, some three thousand miles away. He spent the next seventy-eight days on the high seas with all of the joys and terrors of sailing. He was swept overboard; he experienced fear, hallucinations, and loneliness. He almost turned back, but finally arrived at his destination and was greeted by nearly 50,000 people. Those people were not there to see history being made; they were there because they identified with Manry's dream. "The voyage was something I simply had to do," Manry told the world.[7]

The notoriety and new sources of income cut Manry free from the bondage he had experienced as a mundane copyeditor. For the rest of his life, he lived this new life-style that came about as he was willing to live out one of his dreams.

A man's changed life-style may be triggered by wonderful dreams of faraway places or of experiences he wants to have before he dies. On the other hand, it may start because he feels deprived, frustrated, or depressed. Colonel Edward E. "Buzz" Aldrin, Jr., the second human to step on the moon, in his autobiography, *Return to Earth*, shared some of the positive results of his midlife depression. "My depression forced me, at the age of forty-one, to stop and for the first time examine my life. The circumstances that brought about my study were extreme, but I now look upon this experience as one of the most valuable things I have done. It taught me to live again, at an age when it is very possible to begin anew."[8]

Aldrin left the Air Force and began ranching in California.

A YOUNG LIFE-STYLE

The major thrust of a man's drive for a new body, a new packaging in the kind of clothes he wears, and a different life-style is to convince himself and the world around him that he is still young. He enlists the help of all the experts to maintain his youthful appearance. Bags under his eyes can be removed, double chins can disappear, his face can be lifted, his nose can be modified, and his hair can be transplanted onto his head or chest. One man's hairstylist told him, "95 percent of our hair coloring business today is from middle-aged businessmen who try to look younger."[9] Another stylist figures that male hair dyeing has increased 500 percent in the past ten years.

If a man's purpose in all these changes is to turn back the clock and recapture lost years, he is destined for disappointment. The solution will be incomplete. However, each of these changes, if carried out in the context of a growing realization of who he is and what he wants to be, can have a positive affect on a man's self-image. The changes must be the fulfillment of new or enlarged goals from his young adult life. If the changes are not part of panic to remain young forever, then the new exercises, diet, medical checkups, loss of weight, fashionable clothes, and more realistic life-style will become part of a positive solution in his mid-life crisis.

> Never envy the wicked! Soon they fade away
> like grass and disappear. Trust in the Lord

instead. Be kind and good to others; then you will live safely here in the land and prosper, feeding in safety.

Be delighted with the Lord. Then he will give you all your heart's desires. Commit everything you do to the Lord. Trust him to help you do it and he will. (Ps. 37:1-5)

9
EARLY RETIREMENT

ONE OF MY FANTASIES in recent years has been to gain increasing experience with sailboats in the thirty-foot class and then set out on a cruise to circle the Caribbean Islands. No timetable! Simply go along from one small island's secluded cove to another, living from the sea and foods of the islands. And above all, living without a razor.

THE BLISS OF DROPPING OUT

Again and again I hear men in mid-life talk about what sheer joy there would be in quitting their work. Many men feel their work consumes so much of their time and energy they don't have time to establish their own identity.

Rust Hills, in *How to Retire at Forty-One*, says there are four absolute prerequisites if you are going to retire early: "First and foremost is that you *be* forty-one and have a job to retire *from*. Second, you should be somewhat fed up with your work. . . . Third, you should have done fairly well when you were working so you won't feel your retreat is some kind of a defeat. Fourth . . . you should have some idea of how you are going to use all of the time that will suddenly become available."[1]

Hills decided to leave his job in writing and publishing so he could retreat to his oceanside place called Coveside. He felt he simply could not go on the way he was and needed some time to think things over for at least a year or two.

Hills is careful to point out that sometimes a person only *changes jobs* at mid-life, and this, in a sense, is cheating, he says. "These people aren't *retiring* at all—they're just *switching*. . . . It's like a good second marriage."[2]

EARLY OUT

Early retirement has its own kinds of stresses, especially for the man who has been working frantically and decides to drop out. It's almost like trying to get unhooked from a drug addiction cold turkey. There can be violent emotional convulsions and erratic responses, because the individual no longer has structure in his life provided by the working routine. The person in early retirement sometimes experiences the same emotional stress working people have over long holidays, such as at

95

Christmas and New Year's. Many men feel they are valuable and worthwhile because of their work, even though at the same time they may feel their work is oppressive. When they don't work over an extended holiday, they quite often get the blues because they feel worthless. The early retirement may cause a man to feel that he has the Christmas neurosis blues all year.

THE GURU OF NO WORK

Hills reminds us of Thoreau and his early retirement and points out that Thoreau's observation on work and play was at one time displayed on the advertising cards of the New York City Transit Authority. They read:

> The mass of men lead lives of quiet desperation. What is called resignation is confirmed desperation. From the desperate city you go into the desperate country. . . . A stereotyped but unconscious despair is concealed even under what is called games and amusement of mankind. There is no play in them, for this comes after work. But it is a characteristic of wisdom not to do desperate things.[3]

Thoreau has been idealized by many as having carried out the perfect way to live—dropping out and doing his own thing. Even though Thoreau's pursuits were unlike most men's occupations, he never did truly drop out; he never was able to do simply nothing. Thoreau was always at work. He was an amateur naturalist. He wrote books, gave lectures, traveled, and studied. Thoreau could be occupied for hours in simple observation of the life going on in his pond just beneath the ice. Yes, Thoreau had dropped out from society, in a sense, but he had not dropped out from life. He had only changed jobs.

REAL FEARS

Fear sometimes is the real pressure that drives a man to early retirement. He is afraid of the young men coming up within the company. He is afraid that he is going to be displaced and his information and expertise will become outmoded, so he opts to retire early. It's not necessarily because he doesn't enjoy his job, but he is afraid he is going to be kicked out.

Certainly there are real fears stemming from the rapidly changing technical society in which we live, but a man's decision to quit his job and drop out is simply another escape. There are some partial benefits; that is, he will probably be more rested and will have some opportunity to think through who he is. But it certainly will not be satisfying as a long-range solution.

For most men in our society, their occupation—in an office, factory, or field—is where they gain identity and self-esteem. When a man drops out, he has to establish an entirely new identity and activities that will provide a positive self-image for him. Unless he does this, his so-called solution will only dig his hole deeper.

> In my distress I prayed to the Lord and he answered me and rescued me. He is for me! How can I be afraid? What can mere man do to me? The Lord is on my side, he will help me. . . .
>
> It is better to trust the Lord than to put confidence in men. (Ps. 118:5-8)

10
THE AFFAIR

The French have a word for it: *démon de midi*; the "devil" that gets into men at the "noonday" of their lives when their wives have perhaps grown matronly. The Germans have a word for it too: *Torschlusspanik*, "closed-door panic"; the pursuit of young women by middle-aged men seeking a final fling "before the gates close."[1]

OF ALL THE SOLUTIONS that the man in mid-life may try, the affair is perhaps the most common—at least, one of the most talked about. The mid-life affair is the subject of numerous radio and television programs, magazine articles, and movies. Publishers, writers, and producers justify this by saying that they are only presenting what the American public wants.

IS EVERYBODY DOING IT?

Barbara Fried in her book, *The Middle-Age Crisis*, talks about twelve marriages of mid-life people she knew at a seaside colony one summer. One or both of the partners in the marriages were having extramarital affairs. One woman summarized what was happening. "Well, I look at it this way. There was a year when it seemed that everybody I knew, including me, was getting married, and now there's another year when it seems everybody I know, including me, is getting divorced."[2]

Morton Hunt, who has done a great deal of research in recent years concerning the sexual habits of Americans, says bluntly in *The Affair:* "Many people cheat—some a little, some a lot; most who don't would like to but are afraid; neither the actual nor the would-be cheaters admit the truth or defend their views except to a few confidants; and practically all of them teach their children the accepted traditional code though they know they neither believe in it themselves nor expect that their children will do so when they grow up."[3]

Family breakup through divorce is reaching epidemic proportions. In some major urban areas of our country, the number of divorces granted in a year is greater than the number of marriages performed. The man in mid-life is in an extremely precarious position. There is strong internal pressure to change his own life-style, and he lives in a society in which it appears that "everybody is doing it."

WHY DAVID GOT IN TROUBLE

David's mid-life affair with Bath-sheba is probably the

best-known story of unfaithfulness in the Bible. His affair followed a pattern similar to the affairs of many men in mid-life today. "In the spring of the following year," says 2 Samuel 11:1-2, "at the time when wars begin, David sent Joab and the Israeli army to destroy the Ammonites. . . . But David stayed in Jerusalem. One night he couldn't get to sleep and went for a stroll on the roof of the palace."

David was a man at mid-life who now was too valuable to be leading the army as he did when he was younger. Joab, one of his officers, encouraged him to stay at home. When the battle was secure, he could "bring the rest of the army and finish the job, so that you will get the credit for the victory instead of me" (2 Sam. 12:28).

PHYSICAL STRENGTH—BANE OR BLESSING?

David had lived all of his life by his physical power. As a young man tending sheep, he had fought off wild lions and bears. When he was only a teenager, he had his famous confrontation with the giant Goliath. Goliath's sword, taken as a trophy after that victory, became the symbol to David and to the nation of David's physical prowess.

After he was anointed to be king, while yet in his teens, he was deprived from assuming the throne by the insanely jealous King Saul. For the next ten years, through his late teens and early twenties, David was forced to live in the mountains and caves, depending upon his physical ability, wit, and power for survival.

David's success after he did assume the throne led him increasingly to administrative duties. His success made him more and more valuable and pulled him increasingly from the physical kind of life and existence that had given him meaning for so many years. David was a man who was emotionally set up for an affair. His inability to sleep perhaps had a direct connection with what was happening inside of him at this age in life as he was increasingly forced to assume different roles.

DAVID'S DISCONTENT

Why do men get into affairs? Invariably, a set of circumstances sets them up, like David, and they think of the affair as a way to satisfy the discontent they feel. In the midst of a great deal of internal turmoil and dissatisfaction with life, it's easy for a person to think back over his life and remember the kinds of things that gave him pleasure and satisfaction in the past. A new girlfriend did it when he was a teenager. Why shouldn't it happen again? After all, romance dispelled monotony, emptiness, boredom, and depression. He remembers what it was like to look into the eyes of someone who was looking intently at him. He recalls the thrill of the first touch of her hand. He remembers how satisfying it was to talk to another person for endless hours. Certainly that same sparkle would happen again. He really believes what Americans have been taught—"Love conquers all."

Sometimes the man in mid-life begins to sense an awakening sexual drive. Some people suggest that this may be caused by some hormonal changes. Others feel that since a man is losing his potency and virility, he becomes a victim of fantasizing and daydreaming: "What would it be like?"

The strength of emotion a man feels when caught at

mid-life with this passionate sexual drive is expressed by the character in *The Seeker:* "I had been beset with an intense and indiscriminate lust, a hunger for variety and possession and penetration that would gather up and devour all the women of the world. I had not acted on these impulses, but they had transformed my inner life into a venereal phantasmagoria."[4]

The problem with fantasizing and daydreaming is that the more they are indulged in, the more they prepare the man for the affair. The Bible tells us, "As a man thinks in himself, so is he" (Prov. 23:7, NASB). The man at mid-life, however, rationalizes that he deserves a little happiness, a little fling, so he justifies his fantasizing as totally acceptable. He may even believe that by having an affair he will become a more effective husband and a better lover.

Perhaps the most common cause for the mid-life affair is a desperate urgency to solve the trauma of lost youth and masculinity. One man said, "When I used to pass a pretty young woman on the street there was a sort of electricity between us—a message that I found her very attractive, and that the feeling might be reciprocated. Lately I have noticed that this happens less and less often. *I'm* still responding to them, but now, the younger women especially, don't even acknowledge my existence."[5]

THE AVAILABLE MISTRESS

The man in mid-life crisis is an unhappy man. There is a spiritual and emotional vacuum in his personality. Something has to meet the needs of this man and, most surely, someone will. Unfortunately there are women who also have problems and who are looking for solutions to their troubles.

The unhappy man in mid-life doesn't set out in a careful search for the best possible person to meet the needs of his life. Statistics show that he relates to someone who is readily available. This is why we see the common picture of the office romance. There is opportunity, a shared work experience, and a degree of trust and mutual respect. It is convenient to share common anxieties and stresses. The affair generally starts out with a simple sharing of problems. Then the relationship deepens and moves toward a physical context.

A VACUUM IS DANGEROUS

Over the years I have counseled many men and women involved in affairs. Always there has been a vacuum, an unhappiness, that prepared them for the affair. Then someone has been readily available. The relationship started with light social discussions that became more meaningful as the couple spent more time together.

A dentist begins to spend time with his hygienist, talking about the work at the office and his own personal life. A businessman finds it convenient to talk to one of the women who works in his business. A neighbor begins to talk to his neighbor, and they share together some basics about gardening. A deacon in the church decides to carry out the spiritual ministry of helping widows and so begins doing some of the maintenance around a widow's house.

The list of people is almost endless, and the patterns are similar. One person has an emotional-spiritual vacuum in his personality. He begins to share his anxieties with a person who also has a vacuum. They are drawn together in a deep, caring relationship that leads to an emotional and physical affair. Almost all of these affairs come about between people who already know each other and who have a close, convenient opportunity to share their experiences.

David's affair with Bath-sheba followed the same pattern. The Bible says, "One night he couldn't get to sleep and went for a stroll on the roof of the palace. As he looked out over the city, he noticed a woman of unusual beauty taking her evening bath. He sent to find out who she was and was told that she was Bath-sheba" (2 Sam. 11:2-3).

David had been exposed to many beautiful women. In fact, he had a harem of beautiful women living in the palace. Why was this woman different? Because David was different. David was emotionally prepared for an affair, and Bath-sheba was available.

THE AFFAIR AND THE MARRIAGE

Affairs seem to take one of three general directions. One, the man has an affair or a series of affairs, decides that's not what he wants, and settles down again with his wife in a more successful marriage than he had experienced before.

Or, the man has an affair, comes back to his wife, but she will not really forgive him, and there is no resolution to the problems that caused the marital vacuum in the first place. The marriage may be reestablished, but it is not secure, and in coming months or years it breaks apart again. Sometimes this is the final break; other times it is only one of a series of breaks.

The third direction is that a man decides the new woman is far superior to his wife, so he asks for a divorce. Or the wife may decide immediately that she cannot live with a man who has had an affair, and she asks for a divorce.

HOW SOCIETY VIEWS THE AFFAIR

Society is a bag of strange mixtures. On the one hand, people seem fascinated with affairs; but on the other hand, they are extremely judgmental of anyone who gets caught. Society also feels that if a man in his twenties is fooling around sexually, married or unmarried, he is a swinger, but at forty-five he is a dirty old man.

A number of writers in recent years have proposed a free-love approach to marriage. They argue that only cultural prejudice ties sex to love and marriage, and sexual fidelity is essentially a property right and therefore dehumanizing. If a marriage is to survive, the partners must go outside for a broader experience, enrichment, and growth.

Marriage counselors, on the other hand, generally consider that free love creates *more* problems.

God, of course, who has a fair degree of insight into people as their Creator, planned that husband and wife should have a commitment to each other *only* all through their lives.

As we divorce sex from love and commitment, sex loses its ability to satisfy. Some in our society have become increasingly jaded and need more sex and novelty to satisfy their distorted personalities. From the beginning of life, a child learns that there is a correlation between his sensory good feelings and love. As he grows, he learns that his coming into the world was part of the expression of his mother and father loving each other and committing themselves to stay with each other in order to care for him. In adulthood there are deep-seated, unconscious convictions that sex is related to commitment.

THE LOVER WANTS COMMITMENT

People don't really get what they hoped for in an affair. One or the other, or perhaps both, originally thought that the affair would be just a passing thing, providing some physical release and an opportunity to share some happiness together. The more time they spend together, however, the more the need for commitment begins to grow.

I know two different young women who were each angry at their lovers because these men continued to have sexual relationships with their wives! The men couldn't understand what was happening, but these young women were asking for commitment. I have seen the pattern in reverse, where a man becomes furious when his mistress has an occasional extra affair in the middle of the affair that he is having with her. He tries to get her to stop, to own her, to force her to be committed only to him.

EVERYONE IS *NOT* DOING IT

It is easy to conclude that every man in mid-life is

involved in an affair. That is not at all the case, although the time for most affairs comes during a fifteen-year span from about thirty-five to fifty. Dr. Harry J. Johnson in *Executive Life-styles* said as he evaluated 6,000 business executives, "only one in five married men engages in outside affairs either regularly or occasionally."[6] He also noticed that as income rose, the tendency for affairs increased. Thirty-two percent of the men in the $50,000-a-year bracket were involved in affairs.

BATH-SHEBA HAD PROBLEMS

David's affair with Bath-sheba appeared to be a one-night stand. David saw this attractive female body and wanted it. Perhaps he felt that the novelty would relieve some of the pressures he felt. "Then David sent for her and when she came he slept with her. . . . Then she returned home" (2 Sam. 11:4).

It's important to note that not only was David prepared for the affair, but so was Bath-sheba. Her husband was off at war. She was alone. Needs in her life were going unmet. It was not simply that the king was calling for her; it would appear that she was making herself available to him. After all, she was taking her bath within close proximity of his bedroom rooftop view. This also fits the pattern—the woman who is available for the affair has some emotional needs in her own life that she is seeking to satisfy.

Perhaps the best treatment of the emotional problems of the other woman is given by Bergler in *Revolt of the Middle-Aged Man*. In chapter 5, entitled "My Wife Doesn't Understand Me, Will You?" he discusses in detail several different kinds of women who are available for affairs. The first is Miss Injustice Collector. This is the young woman who gets involved with a married man so she can be involved with an impossible situation and, thereby, prove that life is really against her. The second type is Miss Mild Resignation. This woman has experienced an earlier unhappy marriage and resigns herself to continued abuse from this new relationship. She is extremely self-punishing.

The third type he discusses is Miss Illusion, who is a naive person with a surface sophistication. Miss Magic Gesture is the one who selflessly devotes herself to advancing the happiness of the man in mid-life crisis. Miss Revenge and Miss Professional Troublemaker seem to have a determined desire to break the man's marriage because of their own unhappy experiences as children, especially with their mothers. Miss Rescue Fantasy is similar to Miss Magic Gesture. The last two are Miss Golddigger and Miss Promiscuous. These each have their own unique hangups—the first about money and possessions, and the second about sex to compensate for frigidity in their own lives.

NEUROTICS ATTRACT NEUROTICS

Bergler explains that most affairs with younger women are with those who are also emotionally troubled. "If a girl is halfway stable emotionally, she automatically and unconsciously avoids the rebel's hopeless troubles and the problems arising from any relationship with him. It may be surprising to find that so many of the *young* girls and women chosen by the middle-aged rebel and cast in the role of the understanding woman are psychic masochists."[7] Thus, says Bergler, the mid-life man who is looking for a more ideal relationship than he has in his present marriage is fighting insurmountable odds.

AFFAIRS PRODUCE STRESS

Most American men involved in an affair at mid-life experience a great deal of stress. These men find an intensifying of pressures, even though they might reveal at the same time that there is a great sense of spark and newness that they have not felt for many years. Some men, to handle the conflicting emotions within themselves, almost become a Dr. Jekyll and Mr. Hyde. They take on one life-style and form of thinking when they are with their wife and family, totally blocking out the other life. When they are with their mistress, they become another person, mentally blotting out the life with the wife and family. By this mental gymnastic the man hopes he will not be forced to bring about a unification of his two personalities.

HOW DID HE GET SO INVOLVED?

Another problem is that usually the affair grows beyond the original expectations. It was supposed to be a rather brief, casual, bright interlude in his life, but it has become something more than that to the woman.

It was so in David's case. He had counted on a one-night stand, but then a note was placed in his hands by a messenger. His heart must have skipped several beats and his face turned a little bit white as Bath-sheba announced that she was pregnant. The one-night stand had become more serious than the casual event he had planned.

It is fairly common knowledge that "men give love to get sex" and "women give sex to get love," so the man involved in an affair must, to some degree, convince the woman that he really cares for her in order to have a satisfying sex relationship. Therefore, one of the basic premises of the affair is that he is not buying a woman; he is developing a relationship—which may lead into sexual contact. For most women, a live, vital enthusiastic sexual relationship is only possible as they feel a deep sense of acceptance and warmth.

The man also may find himself preoccupied with this new relationship, so that it takes a great deal of his time and thought. In fact, the affair may be draining more energy away from his marriage and family than he wants. He wanted only a brief affair, sprinkled with sex and understanding, but it now grows beyond his original plan.

DESTRUCTIVE RISKS

Secondly, there are great risks involved for the man in mid-life pursuing a younger woman. She may reject him for a younger man. Society may reject him, even though society is preoccupied and tantalized by such affairs. Then there is the constant awareness that the affair is a violation of God's truth.

There may be psychological damages if the man is unable to carry out a sexual relationship. One man asked me why it was that he increasingly found it difficult to maintain an erection when he was with his mistress. He was worried that he was losing his potency. With his wife he had no sexual problems at all. Another man said that the opposite was happening for him. As soon as he started the affair, he was unable to have sexual relationships with his wife. Both of these men were experiencing some of the risk of psychological damage that is involved in affairs.

Passages calls attention to two of the risks that the mid-life man may face: "Today the silvery-sideburned sexual hunter finds himself in competition with younger men who can pick up from one good porn film the technique it took their elders years to acquire. And among the current generation of young women, he is apt to find an aggressive bluntness that is positively shriveling in bed."[8]

THE MISTRESS SUFFERS

There is also the risk of damage for the mistress involved in the affair. I know of two different young women, both in their early thirties, who were trying to work through such damage. Both of these women had undergone abortions, with a great deal of emotional and spiritual trauma. Neither of them wanted the abortion but felt it was the only way to keep the love relationship. Tragically, neither of these women got what they wanted and only experienced hurt and distress as the relationships came apart.

THE AFFAIR COLLAPSES

A fourth major problem in the affair is that the relationship needs security to continue—yet by its very definition, it is a liaison that lacks security. People having an affair cannot afford for that relationship to develop beyond the superficial. Therefore, the couple involved in the affair often have very limited activities. They are ashamed to let the community know about their affair. They feel guilty before God. After all, you can't take your lover to church or introduce her to your small Bible group or take her home to meet mom. You might talk secretly at a private little restaurant and then go to bed together, but the spectrum of your relationship is extremely narrow and, thus, destructive.

What the man in mid-life is trying to escape is the monotony and boredom of his marriage, but he soon finds that he has reproduced the same tediousness in the affair. The monotony is even more intense, because the affair doesn't have the potential to grow into a broad relationship that will provide variety, sparkle, and, ultimately, security. Quite often when the affair becomes publicly known and the couple tries to build a broader relationship, they find that they don't like each other after all.

Bernice Neugarten, professor of human development at the University of Chicago, has been studying the lives of middle-aged people for over twenty years. She says that intimacy can be quickly attained, but that people are looking for something more than immediate intimacy. "You can go to bed with someone," she says, "but that somehow doesn't dismiss the need for the long-standing relationship; you *still* want to go home to someone who has known you for twenty-five years."[9]

There was a time when I wouldn't admit what a sinner I was. But my dishonesty made me miserable and filled my days with frustration. All day and all night your hand was heavy on me. My strength evaporated like water on a sunny day until I finally admitted all my sins to you and stopped trying to hide them. I said to myself, "I will confess them to the Lord." And you forgave me! All my guilt is gone. (Ps. 32:3-5)

11
ESCAPING THE AFFAIR

AT FIRST THE AFFAIR seems to hold so many promises. Someone is available, a man's needs seem to be met, and, for a time, he feels he is living in absolute bliss. Now because of increasing problems and dissatisfaction, the affair begins to disintegrate, and the mid-life man moves toward disengagement.

David attempted to solve his problem with Bath-sheba by first ordering her husband Uriah to return from battle. He hoped Uriah would spend some time with his wife while he was home, that they would have sexual intercourse, and thus David's problem would be solved. He could then easily disengage from this affair.

But the Bible tells us that Uriah didn't go home: "He stayed that night at the gateway of the palace with the other servants of the king" (2 Sam. 11:9). The next day

David learned that Uriah hadn't gone home nor slept with his wife, and David was upset. He called Uriah and asked him why not. Uriah responded that he couldn't go home and sleep with his wife when the other men were out facing the battle. David invited him to dinner that night and got him drunk, hoping that this would lead him to go home and sleep with his wife. Again Uriah refused and slept once more at the entry to the palace.

DISENGAGING IS DIFFICULT

Sometimes the process of becoming detached from the affair becomes extremely involved and damaging to many people. In David's case, he wrote a letter the next morning to Joab, the commander of the army, and instructed him to "put Uriah at the front of the hottest part of the battle—and then pull back and leave him there to die! So Joab assigned Uriah to a spot close to the besieged city where he knew that the enemies' best men were fighting; and Uriah was killed along with several other Israeli soldiers" (2 Sam. 11:16-17).

David's attempt to disengage from the affair had now led him into a murder conspiracy and to the actual death of Uriah, as well as innocent men who were with Uriah.

WHAT WILL HELP DISENGAGEMENT?

The disengagement process is generally painful for most men. I once saw the end of an afternoon movie on television that was the story of a man who had taken his mistress on a vacation. While there he ran into a close friend of his who also knew his wife. The man in mid-life introduced his young mistress as his secretary who had dropped by for the afternoon to take dictation and have dinner with him.

Later that evening the friend confronted the man and said, "You must make a break!"

"But how can I make a break?" the man asked.

"You must create a situation that makes each of you dissatisfied with the relationship so that you won't keep hanging onto the affair" was the friend's advice.

The situation was true to life. Many men having an affair want out but don't know how. They experience much stress and many problems but are unable to disengage.

OBLIGATIONS IN THE WAY

The problem of disengagement is that usually there is no easy way to become unentangled. Someone, usually each of them, gets hurt in the process. The unwillingness to be hurt or to hurt someone else quite often keeps people in a relationship far beyond the reason that drew them together in the first place.

I have encouraged a number of people to take courage and break off the relationship. Even though these are people who have made a personal commitment to God, I have received some of the strangest replies:

"Well, you see, I have led this woman to a relationship with Christ, and I feel like I would be abandoning her spiritually if I would leave her."

"I've become so attached to her children, and they treat me as their father; I would hurt the children if I left."

"I just can't say to her that I don't love her anymore;

she would be shattered by that."

"I've taken her into my business now, and the only way is that I would have to fire her or offer to buy out her shares."

I have worked with both Christians and non-Christians through the disengagement process in an affair. None of these people have been willing to disengage simply because of the moral teaching of the Scripture, even though the Scripture clearly states, "You must not commit adultery." None of these people have been convinced to disengage because of obligations to families and previous commitments. It is my experience that people are ready to disengage from an affair only as the dissatisfaction level rises so that the couple feels there is a greater degree of stress and less satisfaction than what they had hoped for or than what they had previously experienced.

HEALING AFTER THE AFFAIR

During the last stages of an affair and certainly afterward, emotions such as guilt and anger need to be worked through. Sometimes the necessary healing involves not only the two people directly involved but also other members of the family and friends.

David thought he had solved his problem by arranging for Bath-sheba's husband to be killed and then by making her one of his wives. But David had a great deal of guilt that still needed to be settled. He wrote Psalm 32 soon afterward: "What happiness for those whose guilt has been forgiven! What joys when sins are covered over! What relief for those who have confessed their sins and God has cleared their record" (vv. 1-2).

THE HEALING OF GUILT

David couldn't seem to work through his guilt by himself. It was necessary for God to send Nathan the prophet. When Nathan confronted him, David was then able to say, "I have sinned against the Lord." Nathan's reply from God was, "Yes, but the Lord has forgiven you, and you won't die for this sin. But you have given great opportunity to the enemies of the Lord to despise and blaspheme him, so your child shall die" (2 Sam. 12:13-14).

For David to return to a state of emotional and spiritual health, he had to work through the guilt to its logical conclusion by, first of all, owning it as his own responsibility and, then, confessing it to God. Furthermore, he also had to accept the forgiveness God was offering to him and realize that he was cleansed and forgiven Psalm 32:7-8 show that David did accept forgiveness from God and that he was confident of God ministering again to his life in guiding him: "You are my hiding place from every storm of life; you even keep me from getting into trouble! You surround me with songs of victory. I will instruct you (says the Lord) and guide you along the best pathway for your life; I will advise you and watch your progress."

ACCEPTING FORGIVENESS

In the healing after an affair, many people find it difficult to forgive themselves. They may acknowledge the problem as theirs and may be able to confess it to God and to others. They may also know intellectually that they are forgiven by God. However, until they can emotionally accept God's forgiveness, they will not experience total healing.

When a person is in need of this kind of healing, I encourage him to read through the Psalms and consciously think of God speaking directly to him about his relationship with God. It's a help to read the four Gospels, watching specifically for the way Jesus worked with people, and then to remember that Jesus said, "Anyone who has seen me has seen the Father!" (John 14:9).

As we understand the life, ministry, and caring kindness of Jesus, we see an expression of God's concern for men. Repeatedly, Jesus is seen ministering to people who were moral outcasts and rejects of society. He offered them forgiveness, love, and acceptance. He invited them to become part of his family. The Scripture says, in a nutshell, "So if the Son sets you free, you will indeed be free" (John 8:36). That kind of deep forgiveness, accepted emotionally within the personality, is what David needed to experience. It is also what every man involved in an affair needs to experience.

THE HEALING OF OTHERS

David was not alone in this affair; nor was Bath-sheba the only other person. Others were hurt. In David's case, the child born to Bath-sheba died shortly after birth, and there was shame in the sense that the enemies of God had an opportunity to mock and scoff.

A man involved in a mid-life affair not only needs to be healed, but his children need healing as well. Sociologists now estimate that between 25 and 50 million children will be raised by one parent because of divorce during the first eighteen years of their life. Whether or not the affair leads to a divorce, the mid-life affair is especially hard on children in adolescence, who are learning from their parents the concepts of sexuality, caring, love, and commitment.

Teenagers often feel betrayed because a parent, who has led them in one direction, is himself moving in a different direction. Their concepts of love and trust are often shattered. They may look at love now as a weapon to be used against people. Or they may see love as a trap and may determine never to be ensnared.

The wife also needs healing following an affair. Perhaps her greatest fear has been that somehow she might be replaced by another woman. Her self-image has taken a beating. There may be a period of time when the wife becomes bitterly immobilized by terror. Sociologist John Cuber believes that "the closer the marriage, the more likely an extramarital relationship is to ruin it."[1]

It will help if the wife can keep perspective and realize that this affair is probably just that—a temporary affair that will soon be over. If she can be forbearing with him in his wrongdoing, and if she can work at areas in her life and the marital relationship that need improvement, she will be able to accelerate her own healing through this process of pain.

The perspective a wife needs to maintain is that this is a short-range experience probably brought about by some anxieties the husband is going through—perhaps over his own physical fading of youth, fear about his sexual capacity, concern about his position or status at work, or just the impending awareness that someday he will die. It will help if she realizes that he needs to work through these problems, and even though the affair is the wrong way to do this, it will end as the problems begin to be resolved.

As we know, our society teaches that men are strong and have no need. Yet here is a man at mid-life with a great deal of stress, about ready to come apart inside, and he needs to talk with someone about it. Our culture also conditions men not to be close friends with other men—at least, not to the extent of sharing deep, intimate problems. Men have been trained from childhood to be open with their mothers but not with their fathers. The natural outlet for the man in our society, therefore, is to seek a female to share his concerns. If the wife can understand this and realize that her husband needs a friend to talk with, she can direct some of her energies to graciously draw her husband out. She can also encourage male friends to relate in greater depth with him.

The wife also needs to realize that she is in competition with the other woman. It is an unfair competition, but, nevertheless, it is a competition. The other woman never talks about problems such as the appliances that need to be repaired or the mounting bills. She is not nagging or scolding. She presents a listening ear, patience, and understanding. She is an admiring, appreciating, flattering woman who is often a sharp contrast to what the husband is experiencing at home. If his wife realizes the contrast, she can then alter the way she relates to her husband. She can learn to build his ego as a man, as a businessman, as a father, and as a husband, so that he sees his wife in a very positive light as a helpful friend who appreciates him, not only as one making demands on his life.

COUNSELING CAN HELP

It is important for the wife also to realize that there are

causes for this change in her husband's behavior. A counselor can give her insight on the dynamics of the relationship between her and her husband. The counselor may be able to point out areas in which she can improve some of the things that have disappointed her husband. He may help her discover things that are causing stress in the marriage, so they can be removed. As she understands her husband and the dynamics of their marriage, she may find her husband willing to become involved in counseling.

It takes a number of months, perhaps years, for a man to work through the mid-life crisis. If the wife is using this time to encourage the positive development of her own life, personality, and contribution to the marriage, it will give her a sense of achievement and direct her attention away from self-pity. It will also produce positive benefits when the stress period has ended.

A wife reacts many different ways when she finds out her husband has been unfaithful to her. Sometimes Christians tend to condemn and hold up the moral standard of the Bible—faithfulness, i.e., not being involved in adultery. This standard is absolutely accurate and is, without question, the best standard for the family and marriage. Too often, however, when the wife discovers the infidelity of the husband, she reacts with natural hurt and uses the moral teaching of the Bible as a club on her husband. The biblical standards may act as a security blanket to cover guilt she may feel for having a part in causing the infidelity.

What is needed at the point of discovery and thereafter is understanding and forgiveness, with the willingness to forget. The couple then needs to commit themselves to finding causes and solutions, so that the marriage from then on can be what it has never been before in providing happiness and fulfillment for each person.

HONESTY CAN HELP

The question of honesty always comes up when we are talking about the healing of an affair. There is probably no blanket statement that can be made, such as "Tell everything in every detail," or "Tell nothing," or any stage between. Each couple and each situation will have to be treated individually. Ideally, it would be good if a couple were strong enough to share with each other what had happened, with no lasting damage to either personality or to the marriage relationship. In reality, many people cannot stand that kind of truth. Judith Viorst writes about making her husband promise to always tell the full truth in all cases, no matter how unpleasant—and then she wonders, "How come he thought I meant it?"[2]

It is interesting that many people say they want the truth, but in reality, they don't know how much of the truth they can stand. Some counselors believe that after a man has confessed his affair to his wife, she may be able to forgive but she'll never be able to forget.

Some couples in mid-life who are having a great deal of marriage stress honestly don't want to tell each other how they feel, because they are afraid to rock the boat. As one man told me, "I'm not telling my wife how I feel toward other women or what they mean to me, and she's not pushing me to talk about it either." Each one of them, however, is crying on the inside. They each have decided to carry on life as usual, but they are not talking to each other about things that matter, not sharing with friends, and not involving the children. This couple's choice not to share and talk with each other about what is happening on the inside of each of them is a choice that is pushing them further apart. Each concludes that they really have nothing in common, so why stay together?

DEAD-END ROADS

FEAR WON'T HELP

The fear of making things worse by honesty is a real fear. If, however, there is a basic conviction and practice of forgiveness in the life of each person, the marriage relationship can stand a great degree of honesty.

A pastor friend shared with me the increasing problem he was having with lust as he moved into the mid-life era. He found himself repeatedly fantasizing about other women. The problem became so bad that he decided to talk to a Christian psychologist. The psychologist told him that by the next time they got together he wanted him to have shared this with his wife. My friend asked, "How in the world do you share this with your wife? Do you just walk up to her and say, 'You know, I'm really turned on by Mary Jane; I keep dreaming about being in bed with her'? When do you share this with her? At night, when you're snuggling with her? Over a cup of coffee at breakfast? How in the world can you share something as threatening as this with your wife?"

When he went back to the psychologist, my friend told him that he had tried, but he simply could not do it. The words just got stuck in his mouth. The psychologist said that he didn't want to see him again until he had shared this with his wife. So the man finally took his wife out to dinner, and after they had a delightful meal and talked about a lot of other nice things, he told her that there was something he wanted to tell her.

After several minutes of beating around the bush, he finally said, "This might surprise you, but I'm really attracted to other women. They really turn me on."

His wife smiled pleasantly at him and said, "So what else is new?"

He couldn't believe that she knew he was attracted to other women and, beyond that, he couldn't believe that she would understand. As they talked, they came to realize that each of them was attracted to other people and was sexually aroused by other people. Out of that discussion, they recommitted themselves to a position of fidelity to each other.

Marriage counselor David Mace reports that another fellow said, "I'll never forget how Alice behaved when my sordid little affair with the girl at the office blew up in her face. I knew it must be hurting her terribly—but she didn't whine and she didn't lash out. She sat me down, looked me straight in the eyes, and asked me where she had gone wrong and what this girl had that she hadn't. . . . From that moment the other girl didn't have a chance."[3]

THE PRIVATE SELF

Each one of us has private aspects that we never really share with anyone except, perhaps, God. It isn't wrong to have a private self; yet if this restricts the growth of intimacy in the marriage relationship, it will inevitably drive the couple apart.

Many marriages were started on the basis of dishonesty. From the beginning the couple kept from each other things they were afraid would hurt the other person or might cause the other person not to like them if they knew. Many marriages exist for years behind this unfortunate black cape.

I have lived through most of my married life with a fear of letting Sally know some of my own feelings about our marriage, about her, about myself, and about other women. Every now and then I take courage and tell her a little bit more about who I really am. Each time I am afraid, and on many occasions she has been terribly hurt, but as a result we know each other better and our relationship with each other has improved.

Sometimes it is better that some things are never said but simply laid at the feet of God, where he alone provides forgiveness. Sometimes honesty sessions are just times to unload our guilt and load up the other person with a great deal of stress. Generally, however, I think that most couples could push the frontier of honesty and, by doing that, would find greater healing in their relationship, especially during the mid-life crisis.

The man in mid-life hopes an affair will somehow help him in the struggle to remain young, to experience something more meaningful, to meet at a deeper level of interpersonal relationships, and to revitalize his whole stale personality—and for a period of time, it does. But "the sun calmly continues to rise. And we are all, in love or not, a day older. . . ."[4]

> Create in me a new, clean heart, O God, filled with clean thoughts and right desires. Don't toss me aside, banished forever from your presence. Don't take your Holy Spirit from me. Restore to me again the joy of your salvation, and make me willing to obey you. (Ps. 51:10-12)

12
A NEW GOD

SO FAR, NOTHING HAS HELPED our man cope with this terribly grinding emotional oppression that has captured him like a giant bogeyman in the night. Depression and alcohol only intensified his problem. A new body, new clothes, new life-style, and new job, new wife, or an affair—these proved to be a mixed bag, providing temporary relief, but not lasting solutions.

Now he may try one more solution. If he has been a religious man, he may very well declare that the God of his youth and young adulthood has been ineffective to meet the needs of his life and he may now follow a new god of self-gratification. He may also decide to follow no god by saying that God is dead and he wants to be liberated from any concept of God.

If, perchance, he has been a nonreligious person, he

may conclude that the reason for the emptiness and tragedy of his life has been that God has been excluded. So now he may declare that God is alive, and he may determine to follow him with all of his life.

During the 1960s and early 1970s there appeared a succession of articles talking about the minister dropping out. These articles not only pointed up the impossibility of a minister meeting all the needs of all the people in a given church, but they touched on the personal needs and weaknesses in the man himself. We discovered that the mid-life minister experienced many of the same traumas that men in other professions and businesses experienced. Being a minister did not guarantee that he would miss that dreaded plague.

Many ministers in recent years have dropped out; some are victims of the unbelievable system we call the church, but many others are victims of the mid-life crisis and are unable to share that crisis in a meaningful way with people who would still accept them.

FENCE HOPPING

For example, two of my friends, both of whom were ministers, dropped out during this mid-life era. One of them still has a very vital relationship with God. The other one, however, is struggling with that relationship and at this point is saying, "I want to follow a new god or, perhaps, no god."

What a strange fence-hopping process can take place at mid-life! Men who are identified as spiritual may jump over the fence and become followers of new gods or no god for a time, while men who have been identified as following no god at all suddenly become God-conscious.

It is extremely important for a man to realize that the mid-life crisis is bigger than simply deciding to be religious or not be religious. Without any question, a vital, personal relationship with God provides a stronger basis for solving human problems than no relationship with God, but simply because a person is a religious person or a Christian does not exempt him from problems.

Sometimes wives are easily caught in this trap. They think, "If only I could get my husband to become a Christian and start going to church, then all of his problems will be solved." Certainly, he will have a stronger base from which to solve problems, but he may still have problems. If a person becomes a Christian in order *not* to face his problems, then he probably will be disillusioned and later turn his back on God, saying that God failed him. It was not God who failed, but the man hiding behind a religious experience, unwilling to work with God toward the solution of his life problems.

MAYBE A NEW GOD . . .

This new god is called indulgence. It is the god of pleasure, luxury, gusto, comfort, ease, sensuality—the god of hedonism.

The reasoning goes something like this: "I've worked hard all of my life. I obeyed my parents when I was a little kid, did what I was supposed to do in school, went to church like a good little boy, went to college, got a good job, got married and settled down as society expected, started a family, bought a house in the suburbs, even managed to get a second car. I took out life insurance and started retirement funds. I became respectable in the community, was a member of P.T.A., the JayCees, and the local church board. I worked hard at my job; I'm now vice-president in charge of sales in a four-state area.

"I've paid for braces, piano lessons, four different stages of bicycles, and memberships at the Y. I've footed the bills for all kinds of trips and vacations, and I'm carrying a big load to make sure that my kids get a good college education.

"I'm tired of doing all this. It's time that *I* get some pleasure out of life. It's time for *me* to indulge *myself.* I'm going to follow a new life-style that does not include God and sacrifice. I'm going to start using money for *my* own pleasure, *my* own leisure, to get *me* the kind of freedom that *I* want. I'm going to use *my* life and time and money and energy to get *me* the kind of intimacy and sex and pleasure that *I* want. God has talked to me all my life about serving other people, giving to other people, supporting other people. Now it's time *I* get some of that!"

We have a little joke in our family when a person who feels overworked and full of self-pity says, "I've worked my fingers to the bone, and what do I get for it?" The rest of the family joins in and cheerfully yells, "Bony fingers!" Some men see a direct conflict between a God of self-sacrifice and service and their own personal needs. Because they know no other way to define a relationship with God, they conclude that they need a new god and set out to follow this new god of indulgence and pleasure.

MAYBE NO GOD . . .

The attempted solution may also include emancipation—the autonomy of no God. This is really rebellion. Sometimes it is a passive rebellion, but often there is open anger and rejection.

Ever since the man first heard about God as a child, God was a strange mixture. He was a miraculous person who always did good things for him, sort of a combination Santa Claus, Easter Bunny, and Tooth Fairy wrapped into one. God was always there to help him when he had problems, to give him the answers for tests, to help him win baseball games, to forgive him when he needed forgiveness. But now, somehow, God is letting him down. Why are all these troubles and frustrations coming to his life? God must be dead, or he is so inept he can't provide positive solutions for these circumstances.

This man has a distorted view of God and of God's purposes in life, so when God doesn't do what he expects, he declares that God is not alive. This problem has been prevalent through history. After Jesus Christ was crucified and came back to life, he walked, unrecognized, along the road with two of his disciples on their way to Emmaus. They said, "We had thought he was the glorious Messiah and that he had come to rescue Israel" (Luke 24:21). These two disciples were disappointed because Jesus had not performed the way they had anticipated. Later in the story, Jesus reveals himself to them. In their new understanding of Jesus Christ, they again became his followers, and their whole perspective and direction were changed.

Some men are caught in the same kind of situation. Their wrong view of God and what it means to serve God has led them to be disappointed and, ultimately, to decide that God is not worthy of their allegiance.

They have concluded from all of their religious life that serving God will be rewarded with good. The more a man serves him and sacrifices for him, the more good he will receive. They have not come to understand that God wants a relationship. Years ago, in the Old Testament,

God repeatedly told the people he wanted more than their outward worship of sacrifices. He wanted a heart relationship.

THE PROCESS IS THE MESSAGE

The man in mid-life is caught in the American dream, even in his religious life; that is, God is a person to be manipulated to our own ultimate satisfaction. The man believes the end product is the important thing; the method of getting there is relatively unimportant. However, God seems to believe that the process of moving through life is as important as the end result. So Jesus encouraged us to trust our day-by-day affairs to God, to live life one day at a time, to trust both the past and the future to God. Romans 8:28 tells us that "all that happens to us is working for our good." That means God doesn't avoid pain to accomplish our goal. He uses all of life, including pain, to help us develop our character.

At this stage in the mid-life crisis when a man wants to indulge himself and establish his own autonomy, he will probably continue to say there is no God or that he must follow a new god of his own making.

If he decides to follow no God, the big loss is that of communication with God. Beyond any question, he is in the greatest turmoil of his life. What he needs most is someone to understand and support him, yet not demean him as a man. Most of his solutions to his problems, however, tend to cut off people who could be the most help to him.

Men learn early in their lives not to share their problems with other people. Somehow that is not manly and shows weakness, they think, and at mid-life they're supposed to have it all together. So a man is caught in the middle, even with the solutions he tries. They tend to isolate him from familiar ground, from people who can help and care, and, most of all, from God.

> Blessed is the Lord, for he has shown me that his never-failing love protects me like the walls of a fort! I spoke too hastily when I said, "The Lord has deserted me," for you listened to my plea and answered me. (Ps. 31:21-22)

PART 4 LIFE IS PROGRESSIVE

13
ADULTS KEEP DEVELOPING

WHEN I WAS A TEENAGER, I read several different books about teenage life—dating, sex, career choice, and college. Every summer I went to a youth camp, where specialists helped me understand myself, my parents, the opposite sex, the whole spiritual and emotional development of my adolescence. They told me I was fairly normal but that I was going through the teenage years, and the more I understood, the easier the process would be.

Before I was married, I read books on how to relate in married life and on sex in marriage. I took marriage classes in college and talked to a number of people to get my questions answered so that I would make a smooth transition.

When our children came along, Sally and I had Dr.

Spock, our pediatrician, plus grandparents and friends, all anxious to give counsel and advice. The transition to parenting was not difficult, and most of what happened was what I expected.

In graduate school I learned what to expect in my chosen profession, the pastorate. I had three years of graduate study, plus the experience of pastoring churches while a student. All of this was part of the program to prepare me for the transition into my life's work.

THE INFORMATIONAL GAP

Then a strange silence dropped over my life, like a great black curtain. No one told me anything about what was next in life. I was supposed to know it all from here on. Everything would just happen naturally.

I was pushed out and told that now I was the teacher. Anyone over twenty-five didn't need to be taught any more.

I was also busy trying to win the world, build churches, help people with troubles, and generally become a smashing success. I was too busy to think about my feelings and the lack of teachers and leaders through the adult era of life.

At thirty-five I began to grow restless. I had passed a milestone, and I wasn't ever going to come past there again. At thirty-six I received an invitation to spend a month in India training national evangelists. I spent the next year in preparation for the trip, which ultimately stretched around the world and took three months.

Upon returning to the United States, I accepted the pastorate of Twin City Bible Church in Urbana, Illinois, and I felt I had passed through a period of disquiet in my life. I eagerly jumped into the responsibilities of preaching, counseling, and administration, working with hundreds of students from the University of Illinois.

During my forty-third year the uneasiness began to resurface. I was now in my sixth year at this church, and I found myself saying that I was only reliving the fifth year. The anxieties, the questions, the pressures I had begun to hear as a faint voice at thirty-five through thirty-seven now became a loud, raging chorus, crying out for answers and solutions. These voices led to the experience I described in chapter three as I came to the point of near emotional breakdown.

The tragedy is that no one warned me of any of this. It had been kept a deep, dark secret, almost like a giant conspiracy. As I've watched the lives of hundreds of other men over the years, I see that many men face this same kind of stress; yet, very few people talk about it—at least, no one of my acquaintance. Until recently there were very few books written about the mid-life crisis. There were no popular books circulating on the subject in my circle of Christian friends.

It seems to me that a lot of the pressures I've known could have been minimized if I had known about this time in life. A lot of the personal guilt, anxiety, and feelings of failure would have been eliminated if I had known that this is a normal process.

PLEASE, SPARE ME!

One evening recently my wife and I talked with a young seminary student who is preparing for full-time ministry. As I shared with him some of my recent anxieties, he said, "Boy, I hope that never happens to me!" I asked him if he went through any transition during his teenage years; he laughed and said that he had. I continued by telling him that he could expect to go through a similar transitional crisis in mid-life. Again he acted surprised, saying he thought that after he had made it through those early developmental years, everything had settled down for the rest of life.

It is extremely important that men in mid-life understand the process through which they are going, and it is also important that their wives and friends understand the crisis. The next pages and chapters will explore this normal developmental process and show that the mid-life crisis is simply one of the stages that takes place after a person, supposedly, enters the tranquil adult life.

STAGES OF ADULT DEVELOPMENT

In recent years an increasing number of people have begun to recognize the developmental stages of the adult life. Before this, experts had given most of their time to defining stages of childhood and teen development.[1]

Sociologist Charlotte Buhler led the way in the 1930s in Vienna; then Erik Erikson continued the work in the fifties and sixties. Dr. Levinson of Yale University became the most noted authority recently. Author Gail Sheehy took Levinson's findings and put them in popular form for her bestselling book, *Passages*.

Sheehy divides the adult development era as follows:
1. "Pulling up Roots"—18 to 22
2. "The Trying Twenties"—22 to 28
3. "Passage to the Thirties"—28 to 32
4. "Rooting and Extending"—32 to 39

5. "Deadline Decade"—35 to 45
6. "Renewal or Resignation"—after 45 [2]

In each of these eras we should carry out an important emotional work. During the late teens and early twenties we should move to establish independence, separate from the parental home, and establish a unique identity.

During the mid-twenties, as the young man moves into the adult world, he is involved in a stabilizing process that generally includes marriage and the beginning of a career. This is his first settling-down stage. The young man's dreams begin to come true. As Levinson puts it, "A major task of these first periods is to give form to the dream and put it in one's life, to start building a life structure around the dream."[3]

An unsettled period comes about age thirty. This is a time for evaluation, a pause that provides an opportunity to take stock of where a man has come from and where he is going. The difference between this evaluation process and the evaluating that takes place in the forties is that the thirty-year-old is only beginning his career. He does not have a lot of commitments, and there are ample resources, time, and energy to make a major redirection possible. It is, however, a dangerous period of time also. If a man concludes that he is going in a wrong direction, he may make some rather abrupt changes.

The thirties are generally marked by a second settling-down period, similar to the process that went on during the twenties. "At this point," Levinson says, "he has a life structure that he will settle for with enthusiasm and excitement, or with serious misgivings, or in bland acquiescence. Life becomes less provisional. He makes deeper commitments, takes on more adult responsibilities, invests more of himself in family and personal interests, and within this framework, pursues long-range plans and goals."[4]

During this second settling-down stage, a man continues to build his nest, at the same time pursuing with great ambition the dreams and goals of his life. During this highly active period, he has little time for reflection on the purpose of what he is doing.

During the later part of this second settling period there will be a strong urge toward nonconformity, when he will seek to become his own man. He will cast off images that tend to conform him to other personalities and will want to establish his own mark in the world. Sometimes the people who have been the most instrumental in helping him move up the ladder of success will now be cast off so he can develop his own unique personality.

Another evaluation period comes around age forty. This is even more intense than the one in adolescence or the one at thirty. It is this mid-life crisis with which we are most concerned, and it may come any time from thirty-five to fifty-five. (Generally, however, it appears to focus in a man's early forties.) During this time a man asks all of the questions: "Who am I? What have I been doing? Is what I have been doing valuable? Do I want to continue being who I am and doing what I am doing?"

Following the mid-life crisis, a man moves into a third settling-down period, starting in the late forties and continuing to near retirement. The man who successfully navigates the mid-life crisis will experience an increase in productivity, a decrease in competitiveness, a greater desire to be helpful to people, the ability to enjoy leisure, and the ability to be alone. His marriage will generally become more meaningful and satisfying to both partners. There will be an easy transition to becoming a grandparent and trainer of a new generation. Gould calls this a period of "mellowing and warming up."[5]

Of all the stages and transitions a man goes through in

adulthood, it appears that the mid-life crisis is the most dangerous and painful for him, his family, and the community. Levinson says, "It may take the form of a crisis, in the sense of turmoil, disruption, and dramatic change as we have seen. It may go more smoothly. But at the end of it, the man will be different from what he was at the beginning."[6] The mid-life crisis demon loses its terror as we understand the normal developmental stages of life, and our understanding gives good reason for hope.

> He calms the storm and stills the waves. What a blessing is that stillness, as he brings them safely into harbor! (Ps. 107:29-30)

14
THIS CRISIS CAME TO PASS

THE QUESTION I HAVE REPEATEDLY ASKED myself is, "How much longer do I have to go through this? Do I have one year? Six months? Can I speed up the process?"

While I was experiencing mid-life pressures, I read Elisabeth Kübler-Ross's book *On Death and Dying*. Suddenly I began to see that the mid-life crisis can be compared closely to the emotional trauma a person experiences as he faces death.[1] There are definite stages within the mid-life crisis. I had noticed this pattern with other men, and as I began to experience the pressures myself, the pattern began to take form more clearly.

At first, comparing the mid-life crisis to that of death made me feel morbid. However, the more I thought about what I had observed in the lives of other men and in my own experience, the more I came to see that this is exactly what the man in mid-life is wrestling with—death. A man is facing the death of his physical prowess, in the sense that he is no longer a young man; death of the visions and ambitions of his teens and twenties; death of his hopes and aspirations for great achievement and advancement; death of his sexual fantasies; death of the visions for fame and fortune; death for some of the expectations he has had for his children. Yes, and for the first time, he is facing the reality of his own physical death. As a young man, he knew he would die some day, but it never seemed real. Now death has become a reality. In fact, some of his college friends have died already.

Kübler-Ross outlines five emotional stages through which a person goes as he prepares for death:

1. Denial—"It's not me—it's not true!"
2. Anger—"Why me?"
3. Bargaining—"Can't we postpone this?"
4. Depression—"All is lost."
5. Acceptance—"I'm ready."

With only minor modification, these stages can be adapted to the man going through mid-life. They may be very short periods of time or extend over years. Some may overlap and some run concurrently. From my observation, for a man to make it through the mid-life crisis successfully, he needs to move progressively through these stages and effectively deal with each one.

STAGE ONE—DENIAL

"It's not really true that I'm getting older," a man keeps telling himself. For a number of years I was able to get by with that favorite line that I was only twenty-eight, because I tended to look younger than my age. But

145

the truth is that I am *not* twenty-eight. I've always enjoyed young people. My favorite age group is the college age and up through early thirties. I tend to think young, but thinking young does not make one young. I am really forty-five. A few days before I take this manuscript to the publisher, I will turn forty-six.

In some ways denial can be a helpful process, because it starts the transition toward reality. The more a man denies aging, the more his brain interacts with the concept and prepares him to ultimately accept it. He *is* middle-aged. It *has* happened to him and *is* happening to him as certainly as the terminally ill person is going to die. There is no retreat, even if a man tries a new body, new clothes, new life-style, even if he takes a new job, a new wife, has an affair, or tries a new god. There is no way to turn the clock back and make him young again. During the first stages of the crisis, however, a man will vehemently deny that he is getting any older and laughingly say he is "just getting better."

STAGE TWO—ANGER

A man eventually begins to realize that no matter how much he protests, he is, in fact, moving into the middle years of his life. He is no longer young; true, he is not an *old* man, but he is not a young one either.

At this point, he becomes angry: "It's unfair that intelligence and strength should be wasted on the young. It's unfair that they should have the physical bodies when I've got all the experience. It's unfair that the young-adult period that seems so important in life is so very short. It's unfair that I have worked so hard, thinking I was going to arrive at satisfaction, only to find that I've

146

come up empty. It's unfair that I live in a culture that emphasizes youth, that degrades middle-aged people. It is unjust and unfair that God has made men as he has."

Fate seems to have played a terrible trick on him. This strong, good-looking, athletic young man with ideas, energy, and ambition now finds himself with a sagging body, flagging energies, and dreams and visions as broken seashells along the shore. Humpty Dumpty says, "Why shouldn't I be angry? I've fallen off the wall. My life is broken, and I'll never be able to be put together again."

During this angry stage, no amount of consolation seems to be helpful. Everyone and everything become a target for the venom of the man in mid-life. It is nearly impossible to cheer someone at this stage. We can, however, help the person move along to the next stage by letting him verbalize his anger. We can use phrases that reflect the situation as he sees it. We don't condemn him or suggest a solution; rather, we leave questions hanging in the air to encourage discussion. "I imagine you feel very angry that your body is aging." Or, "I guess you feel angry that Mike got the promotion over you." Or, "Do you feel angry and left out when young women no longer look at you with sexy smiles and they see you only as a middle-aged father?"

The stage of anger is a very difficult time for a man's wife and family. They are likely to feel his anger is their fault. Even though he may lash out at them, his anger is really directed at some unknown force. The man in mid-life uses people and circumstances about him as convenient scapegoats for punishment.

STAGE THREE—REPLAY

The third stage in the mid-life crisis can be called "One More Time." Now his anger has begun to subside, and in its place comes a great deal of fantasizing. "Wow! Just to handle the football one more time. To take the snap from center, to step back seven paces, to lift the ball high into the air, to see the tight end streaking for the goal, to feel my arm sweeping through the air. The ball lands beautifully in his arms. He easily steps across the goal line for the winning touchdown. Just one more game. One more time. . . .

"One more success in business . . . a success so big that everyone around me notices how great I really am—how important I am—how absolutely indispensable I am. One more big success before I step off into the oblivion of mid-life and old age. . . .

"One more time with one more woman . . . the newness, the excitement of a new touch, a new face . . . one more sexual experience before my virility fades away like a wilted celery stalk left over from Sunday dinner."

The "one more" fantasy goes on through all areas of the man's life. He wants one more time with his children when they were only children. He wants another shot at young married life. One more time with the boys out on an all-night bender. One more time camping out. One more time for a mountain expedition. One more crack at writing a book or an article. One more opportunity to make a scientific discovery or to invent something that will forever establish his inventive genius. The list is endless.

The replay stage of the mid-life crisis is really a modification of the denial stage. There is an acceptance that "Yes, I am in mid-life," but there is still the last grasping attempt to turn back the pages of time. A friend of mine, only three years younger than I, recently had a new son—by choice. This boy, who has three brothers who are much older, is the pride and joy of my friend's life. He makes his father feel like a young man again, living in that era of a father with a young child—"one more time."

This stage becomes very difficult if the man has a great number of unfulfilled dreams. If he feels he has not really experienced what he wants in life, there will be a great urgency to go back to enjoy these things. The "one more time" stage may become rather lengthy as a man works through the things he missed in his young adult or teen years. This stage may cause great disruption, especially if a man changes his life-style or decides to abandon his family to catch up on some things he missed earlier.

During this stage, a man doesn't want help, and that makes it difficult for the pastor-counselor who might be working with him. The counselor wants to keep things together; yet the anxieties that are producing pressure in the counselee's life will probably become greater unless they are somehow defused. If a man can identify specifically what he feels he must experience "one more time," he might substitute something that will be satisfying and yet not destructive.

For example, one very conservative man who felt used by his family wanted to abandon them, set out on a motorcycle, and go wherever he wanted. I suggested that some of his desire for freedom, adventure, and risk could be met in ways that would be less destructive to the family structure. Perhaps he could try a series of short adventures—backpacking, canoeing, weekend motorcycle trips, running rapids in a rubber raft, learning to scuba dive or climb mountains. These things became palatable substitutes that met this man's needs and at the same time enabled him to maintain the stability his family needed and that he needed to get through mid-life.

The "one more time" stage is most difficult if a man is saying, "One more time with a new woman." Naturally the wife views this as rejection. A number of women have looked at me in startled amazement as I've suggested to them that their husbands do not want to leave them or lose them, but they simply want a new sexual experience to restore their confidence in themselves and experience something they think they've missed. If the wife can be patient and keep her cool during this very painful stage, there is a greater likelihood that the couple will stay together. If, however, the wife pushes the situation and demands a choice, the husband will probably side with the "one more time" option, and the marriage will dissolve.

STAGE FOUR—DEPRESSION

Each stage seems to have within it the seeds of the next. For example, the first stage of denial helps the man move toward anger. Anger at life provides the basis for him to crave replays. The replay stage is not an end in itself and, in fact, moves the man toward depression.

It doesn't matter whether he has a successful or unsuccessful "one more time" stage, the result is the same—he is one day older.

More than likely, he will become depressed. Now, he is depressed not only because he is getting older but because there is no way of stopping the process. Even his delaying maneuvers have not slowed the grim process of the sun rising and setting on him day after day.

His depression takes on a new dimension. Depression came before because he realized that his body was changing and he was getting older, losing his stamina, quickness, strength, and sexual prowess. Now he is even more depressed when he realizes he is moving at an ever increasing pace toward the termination of life.

STAGE FIVE—WITHDRAWAL

Depression may precede withdrawal, or the two may run concurrently. The man in the withdrawal stage asks, "What is it all worth?" and he concludes, "Nothing!" So he determines to drop out of life.

The withdrawal stage may take two different directions. It may be passive, with a man becoming a hermit—"I don't want to talk to anyone, don't want to see anyone. I want to be totally uninvolved." I have watched this stage in a number of Christian men in churches I have pastored. Some of these have been extremely active, setting the direction and tempo for the whole congregation. As they enter the mid-life era and begin to ask what it is all worth, they begin to cut themselves off from life. They gracefully and tactfully decline responsibility and drop off boards and committees. They quietly move to the back pews of the church and in a few months out the back door.

Withdrawal may affect a man's contact with friends. There is never any time to get together; it just doesn't work out. "But don't worry, someday we'll do it." Withdrawal also makes sharp inroads into family relationships. The husband and wife spend very little time talking. Contact with the children is kept to a minimum. In short, contact with people or life itself is very limited.

Withdrawal may also take a very active form. A man may decide to withdraw from his work and home and start a whole new life.

As in each of the other stages, withdrawal has positive as well as negative aspects. The stages of depression and withdrawal can bring about a healing process by giving a man time to be alone, to allow his frayed emotions to rebuild, and even to allow his body to gain strength.

One man's withdrawal took the form of taking off for a month with the family motor home. He was able to go where he wanted, stay where he pleased, be outdoors, and enjoy nature. He got some time in the sun fishing, and, in general, simply allowed his head to clear out. He took along some music, a few books, and even a few of my sermons on tape. This withdrawal period was extremely important for him, because it prepared him for the final stage of acceptance.

The withdrawal stage may be one month or it may be a year. There may also be a moving back and forth between the stages as a man moves nearer to acceptance. He may fall back into depression or drop as far back as anger, but each of those lapses into earlier stages will become less frequent and shorter. As he meets his needs in each stage, he will grow slowly and surely toward a mature acceptance of who he is and where he is in life.

STAGE SIX—ACCEPTANCE

The movement into the acceptance stage is almost unnoticed at first, even to a man himself. It's like the movement of a wave to the shore. You look out at the ocean, and it's almost impossible to pick out an individual wave, but as it moves closer to the shore, it begins to take form and rises higher and higher. The wave curls over, and the whitecap begins to form, the foam shows underneath the curl, and the water from the shore begins to recede as the wave grows in size and comes crashing. As the wave breaks on the shore and you sense its power and majesty, you wonder where the wave was all the time when it was only a part of the ocean. So it is with the man who is beginning to accept himself. At first, he doesn't see the change, but increasingly there is the exhilaration that he is moving out of the mid-life crisis to a new and productive time.

A man begins to notice that for no reason at all, he sees life differently. Only weeks before he had been saying to himself, as the pessimist says about the pie, "Oh, isn't that terrible, half of the pie is gone!" Now, strangely, he begins to view his years optimistically: "Wow! Isn't this great—half of the pie is left!"

He begins to see his assets and his value. He is no longer a worn-out middle-aged man; he is an experienced, able person! He is able to teach and develop the coming generation. He has wisdom and influence. His family and friends are no longer evil ones pushing him into old age; they are pleasant companions who love and care for him.

He looks forward to more leisure time, doing the creative things he has always wanted to do. He has a better understanding of his physical body, of its actual capabilities, and, without anger, he looks forward to adjusting his activities to fit his real body. He has now moved into what Erikson calls the "generative" period of his life and has become, as Gould suggests, "more mellow." This man is entering a *third* settling-down stage of his life. This is the longest one, and it will be the most satisfying. He will be a very significant, productive, giving man; at the same time, he will maintain his own individuality, identity, and privacy.

WHAT IF?

The question that comes repeatedly to me from men and their wives is, "What if I don't make it through these stages? What if I only go as far as anger? Or depression or withdrawal?" The answer to that question is tragically simple. If a man does not progress through the stages and, for one reason or another, stops along the way, he will probably experience a prolonged period of trauma. There may be recurring cycles of mid-life crisis during the next fifteen to twenty years. The third settling-down stage, which should be marked by a great deal of peace, will instead be marked by unsettledness and continual anguish, much the same as the person who never quite makes it through the adolescent transition into young adulthood. That person seems to be forever trying to be a teenager. The man who doesn't make it successfully through his mid-life crisis is forever trying to be a young adult.

A number of men whom I have counseled over the years have deeply concerned me, because I was afraid they would not make the complete movement through all of the stages. Thus far, however, I have not seen one who has not made it all the way. These men have been highly motivated and were willing to work through the painful mid-life problems.

> You have seen me tossing and turning through the night. You have collected all my tears and preserved them in your bottle! You have recorded every one in your book.
> The very day I call for help, the tide of battle turns. My enemies flee! This one thing I *know: God is for me!* (Ps. 56:8-9)

PART 5
THE WIFE'S CRISES

15
BEWILDERED AT THIRTY- FIVE

BY NOW THE WOMEN READERS are beginning to cry out, "Hey, what about me? I've got problems too." That's true, of course. The woman in mid-life is also struggling with pressures. If she's going to help her husband and be what he needs her to be, she must have help.

One of the hardest things for me has been to watch my wife choke back tears, trying to be strong and carry the responsibility of the family, at the same time trying to be optimistic, happy, and support me. Part of me would say, "That's not fair that she has to carry this load," but the other part of me would say, "I'm sorry; I can't do anything about it."

It is extremely difficult to live with a man who is going through the mid-life crisis. Some days he may act like an adolescent, with great outbursts of anger, or deep depression, or withdrawal. He clearly presents a picture of instability. He doesn't know who he is, where he is going, what he is doing. His values are confused.

Just before his mid-life crisis, however, this man clearly knew where he was going, was strongly oriented toward achievement, and seemed to spend all of his energies in clear-cut directions. Now he is like a sailboat caught in a deep fog offshore, without a compass and without wind to move him even if he wanted to go.

This personality change can be very devastating to his wife, especially if she has looked to him for leadership in the family. On the one hand, he wants to be thought of as the leader; on the other hand, he is unable to function as the leader. He wants her to help him with his insecurity, doubt, and weakness. He wants her to understand who he is and what is happening. Yet he wants to be thought of as the strong, secure, sensitive leader.

Women whose husbands are in mid-life crisis have repeatedly said to me, "It's not fair! I have to continue with the day-to-day responsibilities of caring for the children and the household routine, answering questions of friends and relatives, trying to keep things as stable as possible. Yet he can do whatever he wants. He can be depressed or sulky and totally refuse responsibility. He can get in the car and take off for a day or two, but I'm left with all of the pressures and have to pretend to others that things are all right. I'm supposed to be patient and loving, and, on top of that, I have no one to talk to!"

Because the mid-life crisis in men generally occurs in their early forties, it means that the average age of wives is in the late thirties or early forties. At this age a wife is extremely threatened by her husband's crisis. One wife who was nearly forty told me, "I can't stand this any longer. He complains about our marriage, says it was never any good, that he never should have married me.

I'm not attractive to him and don't stimulate him sexually. He says I don't understand him and that I have never understood him." Her body convulsed with sobs, and tears ran down her face, red with anguish. She had been broken and crushed under the terrible indictment laid on her by her husband.

How *does* a woman stand that kind of pressure? How can she take it when she is told straight to her face that nothing she has ever done is worthwhile? And how can she stand the pressure when her husband, in the middle of this crisis, tries to be young just "one more time" and starts an affair with a younger woman? I have repeatedly marveled as I have watched the strength of women at this age as their husbands try to put a guilt trip on them.

This woman needs someone to talk to. She can't talk to her husband for fear of driving him away at some critical stage in his crisis, but she *must* talk to someone. Most women, however, are too ashamed to talk to anyone, partly because they *believe* the indictment from their husbands. They believe they *have* failed—and, to some degree, they have. None of us is perfect. No marriage partner always does everything right, but the indictment from the husband during his crisis is an exaggeration, filled with anger and confusion. He is lashing out, and his wife is conveniently available. He knows he can dump on her, and she won't fire him like a boss would; neither will she walk off like a friend would. She'll hang in there and see him through it because she loves him.

An interesting phenomenon takes place in the lives of women during their forties. They tend to become stronger emotionally. It may have something to do with their husband's crisis, but I think it has more to do with their own crisis that usually takes place in the mid- to-late thirties. A major event in a woman's life takes place somewhere between thirty-five and forty, and is basically an emotional crisis of "Who am I? Do I like what I'm doing? Is what I'm doing important?" A second major event, menopause, takes place around forty-eight to fifty-three.

THE LATE-THIRTIES ANXIETY

Let's assume by her late thirties a woman has been married about fifteen years. She may be hit with a strong need to reevaluate her life. This is about the time her last child goes off to school for all day. It is not the period of the *empty* nest; it is the period of the *quiet* nest. Yes, there are still children in the home, when they're not at school. She still has a role as a mother, but now there are long periods during the day when the house is quiet—almost deafeningly so. There is time to think of what life is all about.

Quite often she will begin to feel that life is passing her by. Her husband is making wild strides at work, continually moving toward success. Her children are in school and launched toward their own careers. She begins to feel left out, unimportant, and insignificant. Has being a mother really amounted to anything? What does she do now with the rest of her life?

Women express feelings such as:

"All I want these days is to be left alone."

"Lately I've gotten very critical about everything and everybody."

"You'd think after eighteen years he wouldn't have to know where I was every minute of the day and night."

"I'm sick and tired of always behaving the way other people want me to."

"Situations I would have sailed through a little while

ago seem to get out of hand these days before I know it—but I simply think to myself, so what? What difference is it going to make?"

"I have made up my mind it's time I had a little fun— you're dead a long, long while."[1]

At this point the woman may decide she wants to have another child in order to restore her sense of usefulness. There are some genetic risks involved in bearing children at an older age, but in a recent book, *You're Not Too Old to Have a Baby*, Jane Price pointed out that the risks of having a child in your thirties have been somewhat overstated.[2]

SHE'S GETTING OLDER

About the time the children begin to leave home for school, she feels a deep sense of aging. Up until this time she has thought of herself as a young married woman. Now with children off to school, she begins to see herself in a slightly older light. Magazine articles and newspapers don't help. *Redbook* magazine, for example, has a slogan which reads, "Some girls are too old for *Redbook*. 18-34. These are the *Redbook* years." Almost everything huckstered on television uses a young, attractive female to push the product.

It was a good, warm feeling when her children called her mommy. Now her kids call her mom, and she senses that her youth has slipped away. How soon will it be before she is called that dreaded term *mother-in-law*?

The physical aging process and its devastation are heard in the bitter words of an extremely beautiful actress who was thirty-nine. "At thirty-seven or thirty-eight, even, a woman's at the peak of her beauty. After that your hair, your skin, your teeth, your eyes, they all deteriorate. Everybody knows that's true. A woman of thirty-nine's already lost everything worth having."[3]

The woman experiencing this emotional stress is undergoing many of the same pressures we've identified in the mid-life crisis of the husband. She feels a great emptiness and uselessness in life. One husband, speaking of his wife, said, "Her big problem is that she's sure there really is going to be no tomorrow—and nobody can convince her otherwise."[4]

THE AFFAIR OF A WIFE

"All of a sudden, you know, I've noticed that the streets're full of men, the way they haven't been since I went boy crazy in high school. For years I must've been going by them with my eyes closed, but now I see them all right. I hardly see anything else."[5]

This reawakened sexual drive seems to have a correlation with the husband's preoccupation with his career, which may appear to his wife as a rejection of her. Along with that, she senses she's growing older. Her purpose as a mother is beginning to slip. Many of the reasons for her existence and evidences of her self-worth are toppling like a house of dominoes.

The affair may appear to be a way to affirm her own sense of self-worth and attractiveness. She wants to prove to herself that some man will still want her, that her body is still young—and thus, she is worthwhile.

In August, 1973, *Harper's Bazaar* published an article entitled "The Inescapable Threat of the Older Woman," which showed the woman at mid-life competing for and winning men considerably younger. "Mr. Wonderful has discovered the punch of the worldly female ten or fifteen years older than himself and he's been floored by it. So, incredibly, has she."[6]

The older woman is not really a match for the college girl physically, but she competes at a level the younger woman cannot match. "Youth alone is no match for charm, poise, wit, assurance, intelligence, attentiveness and experience. . . . He finds his older lady love all the more fascinating for having *lived*. And when she says softly that he's More Man Than She's Ever Known, he believes it and reaches heretofore-unknown heights in his determination to prove her right, unaware that the lovely crutch of her experience can turn a so-so lover into Superman."[7]

It's easy, when we hear about someone else's affair, to say to ourselves, "That would never happen to me." It's also easy for Christians to say, "It would never happen to me because I'm a Christian." Over the years I have counseled scores of couples where one or both have been involved in an affair. Most of these who are Christians wrestle not only with the problems that caused the affair but also with guilt. On occasion I have asked women what caused them to get involved with another man. Some of these women were leaders in the church, involved in music or teaching, and their response was simply, "I don't know. I just felt something was missing in my life. It just happened."

It seems to me as I compare the motivation of women and men involved in affairs, there are similar causes. It's not so much a basic sexual need as it is a need for understanding and intimacy. Both the man and the woman at different times in their lives are extremely vulnerable to the potential of an affair.

A NEW LOOK

A woman will probably take on a new appearance as she wrestles with this stress time in her life. She'll become increasingly aware of her figure and thus her diet. She buys new clothes to show off her figure and her weight loss, and she may try a new hairstyle and hair color to cover those first tell-tale streaks of gray.

She may become an avid reader of Dr. Joyce Brothers' book, *Better Than Ever*, and she may also seek to become the Ageless Woman under the careful guidance of Gloria Heidi in *Winning the Age Game*. She would do well to balance these with some viewpoints from Christian writers such as Joyce Landorf, who has written, among other books, *The Richest Lady in Town* and *The Fragrance of Beauty*. Although these are not specifically for women in their middle years, there are general principles worth applying.

During her mid- to-late thirties a woman will probably return to the work world. This can be a very frightening experience. She'll be forced to use skills not used for a number of years. She may find it awkward to explain to a personnel officer that she has been busy raising her family and hasn't worked outside the home for twelve or fifteen years. She may be confronted with subtle age discrimination at work, which could intensify her emotional stress.

It is from the crucible of the mid- to-late thirties crisis that we see a stronger, more self-assured woman emerging. It is her strength (discussed in the next chapter), developed through the testing fires of her own experience, that will enable her to help her husband through his mid-life crisis. It is unfortunate that most men are not aware at the time that their wives are going through this kind of stress; they are too preoccupied with their own achievements to share the agony of the wife in her late thirties.

> This I declare, that he alone is my refuge, my place of safety; he is my God, and I am trusting him. For he rescues you from every trap, and protects you from the fatal plague. He will shield you with his wings! They will shelter you. His faithful promises are your armor. (Ps. 91:2-4)

16
BARREN AT FIFTY

SOMETIME BETWEEN FORTY-EIGHT and fifty-three most women experience a second major stress called menopause. There are both physical and emotional changes in menopause, although the emotional stress often begins before the actual physical changes start.

A hundred years ago menopause came basically at the end of a woman's life, but with the increased age span (the average woman is now expected to live into her late seventies), the change of life comes slightly past the halfway mark. She has many years of productivity and opportunity ahead of her, and how she copes with her physical and emotional difficulties during menopause will be important.

Help with physical aspects of the transition, such as cessation of menstruation, hot flashes, insomnia, and dryness of mucous membranes of the vagina, is available from gynecologists. Books such as *Better than Ever* by Dr. Joyce Brothers and *What Wives Wish Their Husbands Knew About Women* by Dr. James Dobson have good information and some helpful suggestions. [1,2]

The physical changes that take place are real, but the psychological fears a woman may experience can be far more damaging to her life as a person. Her physical symptoms during the change of life will pass away, but if she has not dealt with the emotional fears, these may continue for the rest of her life.

THE FEAR OF BEING BARREN

It is strange that many women do not actually want to have any more children, but when they lose the capacity to do so, they feel they have lost some of themselves. If a woman gets most of her self-identity from her role as a mother, she will probably experience a great deal of dread as the physical change of life comes upon her. If, on the other hand, a woman views bearing children and being a mother as only part of her life, she will probably not be shaken by this fear.

Actual childbearing is generally limited to the twenties. By the early thirties most women have decided they do not want to have any more children and direct their energies toward raising the ones they have.

In her forties, her children are adolescents or in college; these are launching years. The focus of her fifties, sixties, and seventies will be grandchildren and great-grandchildren. The time of actually bearing children is thus a limited segment. A hundred years ago the childbearing era was longer and included most of the adult years; today, however, it may be only 10 percent of a woman's life. As a woman sees herself as more than a mother, she will have less struggle with the loss of the capacity to bear children.

THE FEAR OF LOSING HER HUSBAND

If a woman has been highly body-oriented and has felt that her ability to bear children was what kept her husband interested in her, then she may feel that menopause has made her no longer desirable. If she felt she won her husband and held him by the attractiveness of her physical body, then she may fear that her husband will reject her in favor of a woman who is still "complete."

THE FEAR OF BECOMING SEXLESS

Some women mistakenly feel that menopause causes a woman to lose her sexual interests and ability. The opposite is probably true. As the woman comes through her own mid-life stress period in her late thirties, she has an increased sexual awareness and drive. This continues into the forties and does not need to be dampened by menopause. In some ways, menopause actually assists the expansion of sexual interest. After there are no more monthly cycles, no more fear of pregnancy, and no more bothersome contraceptives, for the first time in her life she can be instantly available for sexual intercourse with her husband. This kind of freedom often enhances the married relationship.

Old wives' tales suggesting that a woman becomes sexless as she reaches menopause are just that. As women of all ages have become freer sexually, they have begun to experience a greater amount of sexual satisfaction. This new freedom and sexual satisfaction for women is not because of their ability to bear children, so there is no reason to believe that there should be any diminished sexual desire after a woman has lost her capacity to bear children. Capacity for orgasm has nothing to do with reproduction.

THE EMPTY NEST

The late-thirties stress time was the quiet-nest period. Children were off at school, and the home was strangely silent during the day. With the late forties comes the empty nest—children moving from the home into single life or marriage.

The empty nest is difficult because of the sharp contrast. When our three daughters were in junior high and senior high at the same time, there were always extra young people around the house, loud music playing, extra plates at the dinner table, and both telephone lines constantly in use, not to mention the increased number of oil spots on the driveway from the junk cars the teenagers were driving. When two of the girls went off to school, the volume and the rate of activity decreased considerably.

Even though a woman is extremely busy and many times frustrated with the conflicts and the growth of her adolescent children, yet when the empty nest comes, the sharp, silent contrast will cause her to wish for the good old days, when she felt needed.

169

THE WIFE'S CRISES

Around age fifty it's again important for a woman to put her childbearing and rearing stage into total perspective. She will now probably have as many years alone with her husband as she had with children. Many women think of married life as having children around. The tragedy of this kind of thinking is an unconscious rejection of the second half of married life.

The empty nest may cause the woman to feel underemployed. She still may have tasks to do around the house, responsibilities in the community and the church, but, in reality, she may not be doing things that utilize her full capacities and abilities. A couple should make sure their future plans include full utilization of all the gifts, strengths, and abilities of both of them. If the woman is underchallenged, doing routine, mundane, piddling things that are unimportant to her, she will have a shrinking self-image, less marriage satisfaction, and difficulty moving through the late-forties stress period.

EMPTY MARRIAGE

Some of the marriage conflicts that appear at this age are long-standing problems that have never been resolved, but the wife has been too busy raising children and caring for the needs of the family to be concerned about these potential stress areas.

For twenty years they have done little or nothing to maintain the couple relationship. They went, as it were, from the courting days before marriage right into the childbearing and rearing years, almost to the total neglect of their marriage. Now they sit across the table from each other, wondering whether a marriage relationship is possible. "Can we really be companions? Do we know enough about each other even to live together?" Tragically, some couples in this stage in life decide that there is not enough to work with, and they divorce.

During the wife's late-forties crisis period, the couple should realize that this marriage instability is highly normal, and out of the shakiness of their relationship can come a new relationship that is deeper, more mature, and richer than either of them have experienced previously. They possess a great number of assets between them—psychologically, financially, and in their combined history.

THE BATTLE OF THE MIND

In both of the woman's mid-life stress periods, the big battle is the battle of the mind—what she thinks of herself, her evaluation of her strengths and her ability to contribute to her family and to the community.

"Throughout her adult life, a large part of the identity of the woman who is now in her middle forties has been anchored in her relationships with other people—her husband, her children, her parents."[3] If she derives a great deal of her self-esteem from these three sources, she will experience greater trauma through the two stress periods in her life. Her husband will be going through his own mid-life crisis and will not be the stable person she has counted on. Her children will be establishing their own identities and will need to break away from the close mother relationship. Her parents are in need of more care and, in some sense, the woman in mid-life now becomes the responsible adult overseeing her parents in their later years.

The woman's sense of self-worth must come from within herself rather than only from significant others during this crucial stress period. She should also see her value as something larger than a manager of a household. At age fifty-seven Eleanor Roosevelt wrote, "Somewhere along the line of development we discover what we really are, and then we make our real decision for which we are responsible. Make that decision primarily for yourself because you can never really live anyone else's life, not even your own child's. The influence you exert is through your own life and what you become yourself."[4]

A career, hobbies, or volunteer service at church or a hospital can be of strategic importance to provide a broader base for her sense of self-worth. The sense of worth must come from within the woman, however, and not simply from keeping busy with activities. She must say, "I am worthwhile; I am valuable, not because of what I do, but because I am God's creation, because I am me."

Another aspect of a woman's life that will help her improve her self-image is her own physical appearance. Whether we like it or not, society values a good physical appearance. We have been brainwashed to believe that fat is old; fat is irresponsible; fat, therefore, contributes to a low self-image. The self-image of a woman can be greatly improved as she begins to work on specific projects, including diet, exercise, and proper rest.

Regular exercise can help anyone going through any kind of stress. Physical exercise burns off anxiety, helps a person sleep better, and leads to greater productivity in waking hours.

THE TOUCH OF GOD

There is a depth of self-esteem within a woman's personality that cannot be touched by what other human beings think. Only God can meet her deepest needs. She may not be satisfied by what she does. She may not even be satisfied with the many different ways she is growing. It *is* important that other people encourage her to utilize her gifts and abilities and that she grows in new dimensions, but there may be an emptiness in all that she does because it still does not touch the very deepest levels of her self-worth. Judith Viorst expresses some of that anxiety in her poem called "Self-Improvement Program" when, after a recitation of her many new advances in everything from needlepoint to guitar to advanced Chinese cooking to Primal Scream Therapy, she concludes,

> And I'm working all day and I'm working all night
> To be good-looking, healthy, and wise.
> And adored.
> And contented.
> And brave.
> And well-read.
> And a marvelous hostess,
> Fantastic in bed,
> And bilingual,
> Athletic,
> Artistic . . .
> Won't someone please stop me?[5]

A deep personal relationship with God can provide nourishment for our personality and build our self-image so we can move through any time of stress with confidence.

The apostle Paul talks about the kind of confidence

God can place within the depths of a personality:

> If God is on our side, who can ever be against us? . . .
>
> Who dares accuse us whom God has chosen for his own? Will God? No! He is the one who has forgiven us and given us right standing with himself.
>
> Who then will condemn us? Will Christ? *No!* For he is the one who died for us. . . .
>
> . . . For I am convinced that nothing can ever separate us from his love. . . . Our fears for today, our worries about tomorrow . . .—nothing will ever be able to separate us from the love of God demonstrated by our Lord Jesus Christ when he died for us. (Rom. 8:31-39)

This kind of deep confidence in God comes first from a personal relationship with him. This means we invite God, through Jesus Christ, to come into our lives to forgive our sins, and we mentally exchange our life and its weaknesses for Christ's life and his strength. We receive his righteousness and strength as he takes our guilt onto himself. We now belong to God.

Secondly, this confidence comes from a deep conviction that God deeply cares for us and is moving in all the events of our lives for our good. The Bible says, "And we know that all that happens to us is working for our good if we love God and are fitting into his plans" (Rom. 8:28).

The third concept that will produce a deep quality of self-esteem and spiritual assuredness is the understanding that God is also helping us grow. We have a future. God is not finished with us yet. We are still under construction. There are amazing things yet to be accomplished in our lives. "For because of our faith, he has brought us into this place of highest privilege where we now stand, and we confidently and joyfully look forward to actually becoming all that God has had in mind for us to be" (Rom. 5:2).

Yes, we are in a place of high privilege now, but more than that, something good is going to happen in the future. We don't yet fully know what we are going to become nor the great things God is going to do through us. We do know they will happen because of the supernatural activity of God working in our lives and in the events around us.

This quality of deep confidence in God comes about as we spend more time personally with God, more time meditating on what he has said in the Bible and reflecting on these ideas with God in prayer. We will become like the ideas we take into our personality. That's why the Scripture says to "fix your thoughts on what is true and good and right. . . . And the God of peace will be with you" (Phil. 4:8b-9).

We now have a picture of a woman who can draw on God's strength to give her that inner sense of peace and poise she will need to carry her through this time of stress. A quality relationship with God will enrich her personality for her own enjoyment and for the blessing of other people.

> Lord, with all my heart I thank you. I will sing your praises. . . . When I pray, you answer me, and encourage me by giving me the strength I need. (Ps. 138:1-3)

PART 6

UNAVOIDABLE CONCERNS

17

THE MARRIAGE KNOT

THE SOONER A MAN IN MID-LIFE begins to work on the problems, the sooner he will move through this traumatic time. The two major areas he must work through to successfully make the transition are his marriage and his work. This will consume a lot of his time and energy.

NEW MARRIAGE LIFE-STYLE

Marriage today is different than it was a century ago. Then people married at an older age—men in their late twenties, women in their early twenties. They also had more children, so that children were living in the home a larger portion of married life. Life span was shorter, and people did not remarry as often if one partner died.

Today the average age for marriage is twenty-three for men and twenty-one for women. The first child is born when the mother is twenty-two, and she is through childbearing before she is thirty.[1]

Because families have fewer children, marriages today begin to experience the empty nest when the parents are in their forties. Yet since life expectancy has increased dramatically—both parents may expect to live into their seventies—couples now have half of their marriage without children in the home.

As recently as a hundred years ago, we measured a woman by her ability to bear children, to care for the garden, and to manage the household. We measured a husband by his physical strength and his ability to provide. Love, companionship, intimacy—if they came— were extras but were not the primary targets in marriage.

Our society expects marriage to be marked by love, intimacy, companionship, and mutual happiness. It also expects couples to live in this state of bliss for a longer period of time than any other culture has ever experienced. Some people believe that our expectations are too high and are the actual causes for our marriage breakups. "American marriage has been especially impossible. . . . They set out to mix in one stew what older societies had discovered to be unmixable: romantic attachment, sexual adventure, love, domesticity. . . ."[2]

A man and a woman come now to mid-life, their romantic dreams of endless bliss from the teenage years evaporated; the fascination and novelty of sex have vanished, and the activities of getting a home in the suburbs, raising children, and getting them launched have been accomplished. They find themselves at mid-life with extremely high expectations, but they have done practically nothing for twenty years to improve the quality of their marriage.

NO COUNSEL BEFORE MARRIAGE

Add to the expanded length of marriage and the increased expectations the facts that most couples made their choice of a marriage mate with very little counsel and help. In many of the older cultures of the world, the parents and the community have a great deal to say about this decision. In our culture we allow adolescents, who do not yet fully understand themselves or their own needs, who have had absolutely no experience in choosing a mate, and who may be insecure, vascillating, and immature, to make a choice that is supposed to last for more than fifty years. Premarital counseling is still viewed with suspicion by some couples, and if any counseling is done, it is normally by a minister with little training in the field who spends a couple of hours with them arranging the format of the wedding service.

Many subconscious factors enter into the choice of a mate. Psychologist Clifford Adams lists these in rank order, highlighting a discrepancy between what motivates men and what motivates women.

MALE	FEMALE
Companionship	Love-affection-sentiment
Sex	Security
Love-affection-sentiment	Companionship
Home and family	Home and family
A help mate	Community acceptance
Security	Sex

Dr. Adams concludes that this discrepancy "cannot but lead to widespread dissatisfaction in marriage."[3]

Because I pastor a college church, I am involved in a lot of premarital counseling. I also spend quite a bit of time working with young couples through their early adjustment problems. I often ask an engaged couple to list several needs they feel must be met if they are to consider their marriage a happy, growing relationship. Most couples have never thought in terms of their own needs or of the other person's. They have not considered if they are compatible from a need orientation. Most couples seem to conclude that because they enjoy touching each other, staring into each other's eyes, bowling, and making love, they will have no problems with marriage.

DATING IS DECEPTIVE

The courtship process is basically dishonest. We try to present our best side, of course. We repeatedly work at keeping the other person from knowing our faults, and thus begin a tragic lifelong pattern of sweeping things under the carpet. From this dishonest (but unconscious) act grows a relationship without intimacy.

With all of these built-in disadvantages, it is no wonder that marriages in the mid-years experience a great deal of stress. It's no wonder that some people begin to think that marriage is obsolete and bankrupt. In spite of all the problems, however, there has never been a time in our history when marriage has been more popular. "The content and style of marriage are changing, but marriage itself is more popular than in the past; even the high divorce rate, still growing toward an unknown limit, is no sign of disaffection with marriage but only with unsatisfying marriage, for nearly six-sevenths of the divorced remarry."[4]

Even though the divorce rate is skyrocketing, and even though there is a great deal of stress in mid-life marriages, people continue to seek marriage. "People do not marry because it is their social duty to perpetuate the institution of the family, or because the preacher or Mrs. Grundy both recommend matrimony, or even because they fall in love with each other. They marry because they lived in a family as children and still cannot get over the feeling that being in a family is the only proper, indeed only possible, way to live."[5]

WHAT MAKES A MARRIAGE HAPPY?

A number of factors influence marital happiness. Generally speaking, more education tends to lead toward more marital happiness. This correlation may be true because people with more education tend to delay their marriage until there is more life experience and maturity and, thus, perhaps a better choice of partner.

People who place high emotional expectations on their marriage tend to be less happy in marriage. Those who stress romantic love, those who stress each person becoming unique, those who are extremely sensitive and have a great deal of drive tend to be less contented in marriage than couples who have lower or more traditional expectations for marriage.

Couples tend to evaluate their marriage's happiness differently as the marriage progresses. "Blood and Wolfe discovered that 52 percent of the wives were very satisfied with their marriages during the first two years, but only 6 percent were still satisfied twenty years later and 21 percent 'were very dissatisfied.' "[6] Couples also report an increase in marital happiness after they have passed through the mid-life crisis and the children have left the home.

There seems to be some correlation between happiness reported by a couple and the personal happiness of the husband. "When the husband is unhappy, then the couple is unhappy; but a wife's unhappiness does not seem to transfer to her husband in the same way. . . . Men generally say that they are satisfied with their marriage if their overall life is going well. . . . Marriage is secondary to man's self-esteem but primary to woman's."[7]

Children also influence marital happiness. In the early years of marriage, children tend to build an emotional bond between a man and his wife. During their adolescent years, children tend to drive down their parents' emotional happiness. After the couple has passed the empty nest and mid-life crisis, marital happiness improves with the absence of children, allowing the couple to relate to each other more intimately.

REACTION—FEAR OR HOPE

As I have shared some of this information with couples over the years, they have reacted differently. Some conclude there is no hope for their marriage because of a poor mate selection or wrong expectation or because they have teenagers in the home. Other couples tend to look at the information with hope, realizing that they are not the only ones experiencing marital stress. Together, they decide to work on their problems and to make their marriage more successful.

Beyond any question, we are expecting more of marriage than in the past. It has become more emotionally complex, but at the same time, it is important to realize that God has been involved in marriage since its beginning. He is the one who built the human personality, and he is able to fit us together so our differences don't chafe on each other; rather, they become a means of making the union stronger.

The Bible says, "And the Lord God said, 'It isn't good for man to be alone; I will make a companion for him, a helper suited to his needs' " (Gen. 2:18). When God made Eve for Adam, he didn't make a servant girl. In other Old Testament references the same word for "helper" is used as when referring to God as our helper. God made a companion, someone to share life with Adam. God was fully aware of the complexity of the human personality. These personality differences did not come as a shock to God. He designed us to be different, unique individuals, and he said mankind would never be fulfilled by being alone or isolated. He intended that unique individuals should blend together in a complementary relationship.

TYPICAL PROBLEMS

I have been involved with hundreds of couples undergoing various kinds of marital stress. When they first come for help, they usually report an overall unhappiness and discouragement with marriage, and they may want out. They say they don't love each other. Perhaps there is no sexual relationship, or one or the other has been involved in an affair. They may report physical or emotional abuse, being ignored, or one or the other not carrying out his expected duties in the marriage.

Often the couple will stay together because of social or religious reasons or because they have children at home. They commit themselves to a grin-and-bear-it approach. They communicate, "O.K., I've made a bad marriage, but I'll stick with it, at least until the children are gone."

It's difficult to put all marriage problems into a few easily digested concepts, but the problems do fit a pattern and fall into general groupings.

1. Preoccupation with the process of living. When a man and woman first dated they spent a great deal of time talking with each other and seeking to win and please each other. After they were married, they felt that time spent this way was a luxury. They didn't work on the relationship, but each went about their separate preoccupations, raising their kids, paying on the mortgage, and accumulating things.

2. Lack of communication and intimacy. It isn't that husbands and wives don't talk at all. They talk about many topics—children, money, social responsibilities, repainting the house, caring for the garden. But they do not talk to each other about how they *feel* toward each other and how their goals and aspirations are changing. They aren't sharing the things the other person does that makes them happy or causes them to be uneasy.

As long ago as 1943, David L. Cohn wrote in a book entitled *Love in America.* "It is the rare husband and wife" he wrote then, "who pull up the chairs and spend an hour talking for their own pleasure about non-utilitarian things. . . . Their intellectual and spiritual lives remain personal and separate, with the result that . . . it involves no spiritual communion and no completion of minds. This is a large factor in the loneliness of people. . . ."[8]

A man needs to have intimate relationships with other people. He needs to have at least one person with whom he can be open. He needs to talk about who he really is—his joys and anxieties. Most people expect that marriage will provide that kind of intimacy. When they don't find it in marriage, they feel they have made a mistake. They begin looking for some other person who may be able to provide that intimacy.

As communication and intimacy begin to disappear in marriage, each person becomes more aware of the other's failings. Any intimate communication that does take place tends now to center on criticism and blame fixing. This negative communication and intimacy tend to spiral the marriage relationship into disaster.

In his play *The Bald Soprano*, Eugene Ionesco depicts the same sad state of relationship I commonly see in marriage counseling.

> In one scene a man and woman happen to meet and engage in polite, somewhat mannered conversation. As they talk they discover they both came down to New York that morning on the 10:00 train, and they both have the same apartment house address on Fifth Avenue. To their surprise they discover they both also live in the same apartment and both have a daughter seven years old. To their final astonishment they discover they are man and wife! They live together, share the same bed and the same kitchen table, but intimacy has fled from their relationship, leaving them strangers.[9]

3. Unmet personal needs. The problem of not having needs met had its roots back in courtship days when the couple didn't understand themselves and didn't ask if this relationship would meet their needs. So now they go to a counselor, reporting unhappiness in their marriage and dissatisfaction with each other; their sex life has fallen off, and they just don't love each other any more.

Winch, in a book entitled *Mate Selection*, shows that people are drawn to each other in the courtship stage through unconscious needs being met by the other person.[10] A man may say, "I'm in love with you," but what he really means is, "You meet my needs and make me happy."

People reporting that they are dissatisfied or that they

have fallen out of love are really reporting that their needs are no longer being met. The tragedy of the situation is that one or both partners are unable to verbalize to the other person that they have needs not being met; they simply say, "I don't love you anymore."

A typical example is a husband and wife from another city who came to see me. The husband said he no longer loved his wife but felt obligated to remain married to her because of his spiritual conviction. He reported that they were both unhappy with a series of affairs in which he had been involved.

We soon discovered a very domineering wife who subtly controlled her husband's life and, at the same time, resented his extreme passivity. As a young man he had unconsciously chosen a girl who would make all of the decisions because of his own insecurity, and she had unconsciously chosen a fellow whom she could dominate. As they moved into their middle years, he resented her suppression but was too weak to tell her he now had different needs. His affairs were with women who were less dominant and who allowed him to be more of a man.

This couple began to work on their marriage from the point of view of need fulfillment, sharing with each other who they really were and seeking to meet the other's needs. Strangely enough, they found themselves falling in love again.

Because we are continually changing emotionally, it is ordinary to expect that our needs will also change. Each one meeting the other one's needs is the glue that holds a marriage together. We only understand each other's needs, however, as we communicate honestly and intimately who we are with our partner.

4. *A lack of personal growth*. Old problems from adolescence may still be present. These personal inadequacies can be covered up in the busyness of the early years of

marriage, and if there is no growth, they will likely resurface in the middle years.

A man may have wanted to be married to escape problems—perhaps he was lonely, came from a bad home, felt inadequate and inferior. He hoped marriage would cure these problems. Unfortunately, marriage is made up of the two people who are married to each other, and we each bring to the marriage the problems we have within ourselves. We do not escape emotional problems through marriage. If we were unhappy people before we were married, we will likely be unhappy people after we are married. The unhappiness may not be visible while we are busy pursuing a career or raising children, but unhappiness will certainly reappear during the middle years if there has been no growth.

Boredom with marriage is a common report. Boredom is often directly related to a lack of growth. The word *bore* means to "tire with emptiness or tedium." The human personality enjoys a certain degree of sameness, habit, and routine. These provide security. However, the human personality also needs variation, novelty, and change. These dimensions stimulate and cause the personality to grow.

God has designed the human personality with a great potential for growth. If both people in the marriage are growing, there should never come a time when they know all there is to know about each other. Their relationship will remain fresh, and there won't be the likelihood of boredom.

Some individuals complain that they have lost their identity; they no longer feel like persons who are individual and unique. One man said, "I actually had zero-identity apart from her. . . . I just instinctively did it her way because I was part of her and she was part of me."[11]

Occasionally one of the partners will not allow the

other one to grow because the first one feels insecure. One wife during mid-life felt she needed to return to school and become more involved in community activities as a leader. The growth and aggressiveness of the wife caused her husband to feel very insecure. He selfishly forced her into a role of caring only for the household, the children, and his needs. The pressure from the husband caused greater marital friction and, ultimately, resulted in a breakup and divorce.

Each person needs to grow and encourage the growth of the other. They each need to work at communication and meeting their mate's needs, so their marriage can become a source of strength rather than a drag.

> But Lord, you are my shield, my glory, and my only hope. You alone can lift my head, now bowed in shame. (Ps. 3:3)

18
IN LOVE AGAIN

THE AUTHORS OF THE BOOK *The Dance-Away Lover* say there are three cycles in most marriages: falling in love, falling out of love, and falling back in love. They say that the last cycle is the most difficult, but it is the most rewarding.[1]

Falling in love again will not be like the adolescent experience. The man in mid-life will need to work at it. This new relationship will have deeper dimensions and more lasting qualities than the first time around, but it will require a deep commitment to each other and a willingness on the part of both to work through problems.

TIME

The first requirement of marriage renewal is time. Time alone is difficult to find in the busy mid-life. Careers are usually the most demanding at this era in life. Adolescent children need additional time. The community is calling on the couple for their leadership and involvement. Privacy is almost an impossibility.

If renewal in a marriage is to come about, however, there must be time when a couple can be alone to rekindle the dying fire. It's not enough to say, "Too bad, the fire is going out." You need time to rebuild the fire. New pieces of wood need to be added; the old coals need to be stirred; and probably you will need to get down on your hands and knees and blow on the embers. But, finally, a small flame leaps up through the new wood, and you can begin to enjoy the warmth and fascination of the fire.

The lack of time becomes an excuse a couple uses not to work on renewing their marital fire. A man says the pressure of business is too demanding to have time to work on the marriage. A weekend away at a motel or at a marriage conference, reading a book together, talking to each other in a restaurant late at night are some rekindling activities. All of these take time, and many times the couple won't stop running in order to spend the time to rekindle their fire. The real reason behind not being able to find time may be that the couple does *not want* to rekindle the fire. We always seem to find time to do what we want to do. Unfortunately, one member may have given up hope, thinking that the marriage is beyond the point of being salvaged or that the partner will never meet his needs.

A marriage counselor can often help to reestablish hope so that both partners are then willing to give time for renewal. Sometimes talking to another couple or sharing some marriage stresses in a small group can also bring about hope so that the couple is willing to give the essential ingredient of time for renewal.

COMMITMENT

A second essential ingredient for renewal is commitment. Both people must *want* the marriage to be renewed if it is really to happen. It is common to see one partner come for help, but the other partner, unfortunately, is not interested. Sometimes it's helpful to work with the one partner who is willing to grow so that he or she begins to meet the needs of the partner more completely. Often these changes give hope to the unwilling partner and bring a willingness to work on renewal.

It is ultimately true that if both partners do not work on the marriage, it probably will not be renewed but will, instead, continue to fall apart. One of the partners may say, "My husband (or wife) will never come to see you for help."

"All right," I respond, "let's work with you and bring about your spiritual and emotional growth so that you become an effective mate. I'm hoping your growth will cause a change in your mate's attitude. If it doesn't, you've not lost anything. You will be a happier person because of your growth. If your marriage does fall apart, you will be better able to cope with the breakup, and your potential for relating to people in the future will have been vastly improved."

Commitment also means a willingness to understand the other person and his unique personality. There must be a desire to see his needs and understand what will help him enjoy life more completely.

Commitment means working with the here and now, not the past nor the future. The here and now means the real person to whom you are married. Some people, unfortunately, try to make their mate into the ideal person, or they try to turn time backward to an earlier day. All of these attempts are unrealistic and are guaranteed to fail. The commitment must be to work with this particular person, at this age in life, in the society in which we live.

Commitment means we are willing to fight with each other—willing to express who we are, how we feel, what upsets us. We also commit ourselves to allow the other person to express who he is. Too often, people withdraw when stress begins to appear. I tend to react this way; I stick my head in the sand, hoping the storm will blow over. This doesn't really resolve problems; it only delays them.

There is great benefit as we pass through the conflict barrier and experience the tranquility on the other side.

> On the other side of this conflict lies the relief, security, and comfort of being stark-naked to at least one person in life before whom we can take off our masks, shed our psychological figleaf, and not have to pretend anymore. Such a relationship with a marriage partner can enable me to move more easily with others because someone knows my faults and still accepts me and cares for me, as well as frees me to realize my greater potential because I am not hung up on feeling guilty or stupid.[2]

The book *The Intimate Enemy* teaches a couple how to fight fairly. It also shows them the benefits of this honest relationship. "We have discovered," it says, "that couples who fight together are couples who stay together—provided they know how to fight properly."[3]

FORGIVENESS

A third essential ingredient to a man's marriage renewal is forgiveness. But forgiveness is only one side of the coin; the other side is confession. It is fascinating to me that the New Testament has many accounts of people being alienated from God and people sinning. There are large and repeated discussions on how people should relate to each other, and there are extensive teachings on forgiveness and confession. Yet most married couples feel they are failing if they need to confess *anything* or if they need to forgive each other. Forgiveness and confession ought not to be abnormal experiences. It should be expected that every day there will be *something* we need to confess and *something* we need to forgive.

It is more common to find in marriage that, instead of confessing faults, each partner is trying to fix blame. Blame fixing is a way of trying to guarantee our rights, to make sure we are not mistreated, and also to make sure the other person is properly punished. Blame fixing also tends to focus the attention on the other person and his faults rather than on our faults and our contribution to marital conflict. Blame fixing is likely to be an escape where we can pass off our failures as the ultimate responsibility of the *other* person. This is exactly what Adam did with God in the Garden of Eden. He said, in essence, "Yes, I've sinned, but I would not have sinned if it hadn't been for the woman *you* gave me." This was supposedly to get him off the hook by diverting attention.

However, when a couple commits themselves to forgiveness and confession, their concentration moves totally away from fixing blame. The Bible says in James, "Admit your faults to one another and pray for each other so that you may be healed" (James 5:16). Confession should be a routine part of our life together.

The Scripture also speaks of the other side of the coin—forgiveness. "Stop being mean, bad-tempered and angry. Quarreling, harsh words, and dislike of others should have no place in your lives. Instead, be kind to each other, tenderhearted, forgiving one another, just as God has forgiven you because you belong to Christ" (Eph. 4:31-32).

Forgiveness does not mean delayed retaliation! When we forgive someone, we commit ourselves never to bring this up again. We commit ourselves never to use this as a club on the other person. One wife came to me and told me she was involved with another man. She wanted out, and she wanted help with the causes so this would never happen again. She made the break completely from the other man and began to work on her own marriage. As part of this process, she told her husband about the affair and asked his forgiveness. She also told him that she was lonely and needed his time and love.

The husband was uncomfortable as we talked about how he could help his wife and strengthen their marriage. His feeling was that she got involved in the affair by her own choice and that he was totally without fault.

I told him that he had two choices. One choice was divorce, and he certainly had legal and scriptural grounds for that. The *only* other choice he had was to forgive her and to work on the marriage relationship. No other option would really work.

He said he would forgive her, and for the first few weeks he did work at building the marriage. Before a month had gone by, however, it was evident that he had not really forgiven but had taken a middle road of holding her past sin over her head, using it as a club to force her to do what he wanted. This attitude drove them apart, and they finally divorced.

The basis of our forgiving each other is not that the other person is worthy of being forgiven, nor do we forgive because we are such marvelous people ourselves. Our basis is because God has forgiven us and, therefore, we are *obligated* to forgive each other. In fact, as we repeat the Lord's Prayer, we are saying to God, "Forgive me to the same degree that I am willing to forgive someone else."

In the Old Testament, in the Book of Job, we learn the results of forgiveness. Job's three friends had been criticizing him unjustly. As the story moves along, we realize that all of Job's friends were dead wrong. The Bible doesn't say these men came forward and apologized to Job, but we see Job forgiving them, and we see the result of his forgiveness. "Then, when Job prayed for his friends, the Lord restored his wealth and happiness!" (Job 42:10).

There is a release inside ourselves as we forgive someone else. As we let go of the anger and hostility, we experience a tranquility and happiness. The purpose of our forgiving others is not only to let the other person off the hook so he can begin to heal, but it is also to drain off the anger and hostility within our personality so we can experience the emotional freedom we need.

We may say, "I know I should forgive, but why can't I?" We may not be able to forgive because we have been hurt very deeply. Forgiveness really demands that we draw on the strength of God. If we have been deeply hurt, we need to let God heal that hurt so we can have the capacity to forgive. We may have trouble forgiving because we feel that if we do, the person will go out and do the same dumb thing again. We feel the other person should be punished, and our lack of forgiveness is part of that punishment. We will, however, be able to forgive the other person by yielding the whole punishing process to the justice of God and trusting him to do what is right.

Marriage renewal cannot effectively take place without confession and forgiveness being exercised regularly on the part of each partner. God can help us be open to our need for confession, and we can draw on him for the ability to forgive our mate.

ACCEPTANCE

A fourth requirement for marriage renewal is that we accept each other. The Bible says, "Be humble and gentle. Be patient with each other, making allowance for each other's faults because of your love" (Eph. 4:2). We don't grit our teeth and simply endure the other person's strange thought patterns and ways of behaving; rather we completely accept the other as he is.

The Scripture clearly teaches that each person is unique. Scripture also shows that this uniqueness is going to be abrasive. We will need to be humble, gentle, and patient with each other. If there is going to be healing in a marriage relationship, we must accept the other person as unique. And, more than that, we must accept the person as he *really* is.

Recently a woman shared with me that she longed for her husband to carry some leadership in the home and to minister to her spiritually. She had nagged him for years about these two areas, and he had faithfully resisted so that they achieved an effective stalemate. Finally, the wife came to the point where she could trust the matter into God's hands and told her husband that. She really did back off, allowing him to develop—not from her nagging, but from the quiet prodding of the Holy Spirit.

Several weeks later he called her from his office and said that he had been reading his Bible and wanted to share a verse of Scripture with her that had been meaningful to him. The wife was astounded with joy. The drastic change had come about when she was willing to accept her husband where he was and free him so he could grow at God's pace that was right for him.

SUPPORT

A fifth dimension of marriage renewal is learning to support one another and to carry each other's load. In Galatians there are instructions about this: "Dear brothers, if a Christian is overcome by some sin, you who are godly should gently and humbly help him back onto the right path, remembering that next time it might be one of you who is in the wrong. Share each other's troubles and problems, and so obey our Lord's command" (6:1-2).

Each of us are, from time to time, overloaded with pressures and failures. The responsibility of a friend or mate is to share these troubles and help carry the load.

Learning to support each other and carrying each other's load is a fine art. We may be too embarrassed to ask for help or to let anyone know we have needs. This is unfortunate, because we miss the opportunity of being helped, and we may wrongfully accuse our mate of not caring, when the problem was that there was no communication of need. Men especially are unwilling to share that they have needs. Sometimes they feel they will be less than men if they ask for help.

Jesus, with all of his strength, repeatedly allowed us to see his human side. He allowed people to minister to him. He allowed his disciples to carry out ministries he could easily have carried out himself. He set a pattern by sharing his ministry and his burdens with his disciples.

There is an old story about a farm couple who learned how to signal each other when they needed some encouragement. If the man needed some TLC (tender, loving care), he would walk into the kitchen and toss his hat on the table. This was a signal to his wife that she needed to encourage and strengthen him. If the husband came in from the field and saw his wife wearing her apron backwards, this was a sign that he needed to bear some of her burdens. You guessed it! One day he walked in from the field and threw his hat on the table—and she had her apron on backwards. When a couple has been practicing encouraging and supporting one another—even when they both need help at the same time—they can, in the midst of their need, put their arms around each other and cry together, each receiving strength from the other.

Sometimes one will see the other in need and take advantage of that opportunity to get the upper hand in a power struggle. By deliberately withholding help, a person may feel superior, and the weak person is further weakened. What is really happening is that the mate who is stronger at the time is allowing the other mate to have his emotional legs cut off. The strong mate stands next to the wounded mate and says, "See how tall I am." It's a rather sick and brutal process; yet it goes on repeatedly within some homes. The Bible says very simply, "If anyone thinks he is too great to stoop to this [helping another], he is fooling himself. He is really a nobody" (Gal. 6:3).

LOVE

The last important ingredient for marriage renewal is that the partners must learn to love each other. Earlier we noticed that people say they love each other when they really mean the other person meets their needs. That is not true love or genuine caring for the other individual, but rather it is self-fulfillment.

Ephesians gives us a broader definition of love than simple need fulfillment: "Follow God's example in everything you do just as a much loved child imitates his father. Be full of love for others, following the example of Christ who loved you and gave himself to God as a sacrifice to take away your sins. And God was pleased, for Christ's love for you was like sweet perfume to him" (5:1-2).

We express love to our mate by following God's example of loving us. We also express love toward our mate as we follow the way God's Son, Jesus Christ, loved us and was willing to die on the cross as a substitute for us. That kind of sacrificial love is the quality of caring that is to exist between a husband and wife if there is really to be marriage renewal.

To love a person with the intensity with which God loves us means that we must know that person. We must know who he is and what his needs and aspirations are. We must know how to love him so he will sense he is being loved.

A contractor who had been referred by another counselee came into my office one day. He didn't know what to do, because his wife had walked out on him right after he had given her a birthday present. He had come home in the middle of the day to their new house with all the latest gadgets, thick wall-to-wall carpeting, and plush furniture. He greeted his wife with "Happy Birthday!" and gave her the keys to a new car. When she looked confused, he told her the keys were to the new Cadillac Coupe de Ville he had bought for her birthday. She immediately threw the keys into the thick plush carpet, stomped upstairs, packed her suitcase, and walked out. He couldn't understand what had happened.

After a few weeks, she was willing to come to my office with her husband for counseling. When she was sure I was not her enemy nor her husband's ally, she turned on her husband in a rage I'm sure he had never seen before. She said, "You have bought me all kinds of things all our lives! They were always things *you* thought I wanted! You have never really known *me* as a person. I wouldn't care if we lived in an old house and had a beat-up, old car as long as you spent some time with me. But you are so busy trying to impress everybody with the things you buy for me that you don't have any time to spend with me. All I want is to spend time with you!"

It is impossible to love someone unless you know their needs. This husband certainly was expressing love to his wife from his point of view, but he did not understand his wife's needs, and, as a result, he really did not love her. His love was like the child's love when he gives his father a toy truck at Christmas. God's love is effective for us because he understands our needs and loves us at the point of *our* need.

After we understand the needs of the other person, we must be willing to give energy from our own lives to meet those needs. To understand the other person's needs and not meet those needs cannot be considered love. The apostle James told the story of a man who expressed his need for food to another friend. That friend gave him a spiritual blessing with words only and sent him away. James criticized that action, even though they were nice words, and he pointed out that the need of the man was not met. The verbal expression of caring was useless, because love was not directed to the need.

PRACTICAL STEPS TOWARD RENEWAL

There are some practical steps a man can take toward rebuilding his marriage relationship. First, he can begin to consciously think of looking through his wife's eyes. What does she see when she looks at him? What do his actions show? What does she see as her goals and purpose in life? What stresses and anxieties does she see? As he begins to look through her eyes, life in their marriage will take on different dimensions.

Secondly, a man should begin a deliberate program of building the emotional self-image of his wife. At least once a day he should think of some concrete thing for which he can compliment her. Hopefully, after a few weeks, building up his wife will become a habit. At first, the congratulations and expressions of praise to his wife will probably center around the things she does, but as the weeks go along, the process of building her should move toward praising her for qualities within her personality, such as, "Thank you for being the kind of person who understands me. . . . Thank you for being patient. . . . I'm really grateful that you're a praying woman. . . . Thank you for the great qualities you've instilled in our children. . . . You have a good counseling heart." Praise of her personality will cause more rapid growth than praise of her activities. Emphasize who she is, not what she does.

Next, a man might agree to carry out specific contracts with his wife. This process might be helpful to get them moving toward meeting each other's needs. It will also be a tangible way to measure their success.

For example, one husband complained that his wife was not interested in sex; she complained that he was not interested in doing anything around the house. They worked out a simple contractual agreement under which the husband did some of the jobs his wife had been wanting done, and in return, she was more responsive sexually. As a result, they each felt that their marriage relationship was more meaningful. She saw his concern for keeping things up around the house as a part of his love and care for her, so it was easier to be sexually warm to him. Her sexual responsiveness made him feel like caring for her in tangible ways.

Finally, a man and his wife should sit down with the calendar and plan specific times when they will have special fun activities together. There should be a great variety of events, some taking a whole weekend and others for a shorter period of time. For example, a couple might plan to do something major once every two months, such as a weekend away at a motel, camping out, or a special trip. In between they should plan dates that include activities such as a movie, dinner, or biking, and smaller things such as a walk around the block, a cup of coffee together after supper, or listening to the same song on the radio and each sharing its significance. They may plan some project or hobby that they carry out together. The point is, they should not say to themselves, "Some day we're going to do that"; they should sit down with a calendar and begin to outline *when* they are going to do those things.

I firmly believe in the power of God and the absolute possibility of marriage renewal. I also know that marriage renewal does not usually come about by a simple one-two-three formula unless there is a deep commitment on the part of each person to follow the positive directives God has clearly established in the Scriptures.

> Blessings on all who reverence and trust the Lord—on all who obey him!
> Their reward shall be prosperity and happiness. Your wife shall be contented in your home. And look at all those children! There they sit around the dinner table as vigorous and healthy as young olive trees. That is God's reward to those who reverence and trust him. (Ps. 128:1-4)

19
A SEXY MARRIAGE

DURING THE MID-LIFE CRISIS, a man's sexual capacity is his single greatest concern. Often he is afraid he is losing his sexual ability. The drama goes something like this: a man is overextended at work. He is running out of energy. Younger men seem eager to take his place. He is on innumerable boards and committees for the community and the church. His family has giant financial needs, and there never seems to be enough money to go around. With that as a background, he crawls into bed at night. His wife is experiencing a new sexual awakening. Instead of being passive, she begins aggressive sexual moves on him. To his amazement, he finds he is extremely slow in being ready for the sex act. Partway through intercourse, he may lose his erection, and at that moment, he suddenly believes life is all over. He is no longer a man. It's exactly as he had heard—the middle years mean the end of sex.

As he rolls over and drops off into a fitful sleep, he wonders if the problem is really his or if his wife has lost her ability to stimulate him. For a moment, there is a glimmer of hope. Maybe he is a man still capable of sexual relationships. That's it, he thinks—it's all his wife's fault. Unfortunately he knows very little about male sexual functioning. He does not realize that the problem is not with his wife but with him. The solutions he will try, sad to say, will probably increase his problems with his self-image.

People in mid-life today are a new generation. If a mid-life couple fifty years ago engaged in sex frequently (that is, two or three times a week), they were considered abnormal. If they talked about it, they certainly were perverted.

Today, however, with extended life and improved health, sexual relationships in mid-life can be the best of any era. The mid-life woman has experienced a great deal of sexual freedom, and she has a stronger sex drive than many college-age women. At the same time, her husband has learned a great deal about caring, so that intercourse becomes a deep expression of the relationship rather than simply animal sex. Also, because he is now a mature man, he is better able to control an ejaculation, and thus both of the partners will experience a greater ecstasy in sex than many younger couples experience.

There are, however, problems with the mid-life sexual relationships. An effective and meaningful sexual liaison in mid-life is only possible as the rest of the marriage is going smoothly. If the couple is struggling in several other areas, their sex life will indicate that. Sexual relationships become a sort of barometer, indicating how well other areas of life are functioning.

There was a time when most of the sexual complaints came from men. They complained that their wives were frigid, unresponsive, disinterested in sex. Now an increasing number of wives complain that their husbands are not meeting their sexual needs. The sexual revolution has made it acceptable for a woman to respond the way God made her. Previously a woman felt she had to suppress her feeling of excitement during the sex act. She also had to suppress her aggressiveness. A good girl never initiated sexual relationships. Sex was something good girls never thought about. Now a new door of sexual experience has been opened for women.

A PROBLEM FOR MEN

This new freedom for women, however, places a greater burden on men. Previously men thought that it was their wife's fault when they didn't have sexual relationships; now men are surprised to find that women are extremely interested in sex and can experience orgasm after orgasm in one sexual encounter, perhaps far outdoing their husbands. A man is startled to learn that the ability of his wife to enjoy sex and to respond enthusiastically is basically his responsibility. Many men are not prepared to assume this kind of sexual leadership; they are, in fact, intimidated by the desires and ability of their wife.

A direct negative result of the greater sexual freedom of women and the emotional intimidation experienced by men because of women's freedom may be the strong move toward homosexuality and surgical sex changes. Reportedly, some ten thousand men have indicated a desire to have their sex changed surgically. However, for the man who understands his wife and what is happening in her life, as well as his own, this can be a new day of openness and joy that married life has never before experienced.

It is a great encouragement to me as a pastor-counselor to see the increased openness regarding sex. The Bible has never been silent on the subject and has never treated sex as dirty; sex has always been a gift of God. The Bible has always been more open on the subject than our culture has been.

The sexual revolution, however, not only opened the door for sexual communication, but it also moved increasingly toward distortions. Good sexual relationships might be compaied to rowing a boat. Both oars need to be used at the same time and matched in strength. In our society today, we have overemphasized the physical aspect of sex—the biological, animal dimension—and we have ignored the qualities of love, commitment, warmth, and fidelity. As a result, a sexual partner is often thought of as an "it."

Beyond any question, sex is physical. But the physical part, as one oar of the boat, will only cause the boat to go around in circles, never achieving a goal or a direction. The other oar of the boat is that emotional dimension of understanding and caring for the other person. It is having a depth relationship such as we saw in the previous chapter—spending time with the person, committing oneself to the mate, forgiving, accepting, supporting, and loving that one. This is the other oar of the sexual experience that gives meaning to the physical dimension. Sex is not simply an isolated physical act enjoyed off and on during a week; it is a continued demonstration of caring for each other, expressed by words, togetherness, and prayer as well as in intercourse.

IS THERE SEX AFTER FORTY?

Sometimes the problem with a man at mid-life is that he comes with attitudes from his youth that convince him that sex is over by age forty. Studies of college students show the distorted view of sex activity that is held by many young adults.

A study reported in *Psychology Today* revealed that 646 Illinois State University students felt that their parents "had intercourse once a month or less, never had intercourse before they were married, [and] never had oral-genital sex."

The students seemed to have great trouble accepting the reality of their parents' sex life, and "90 percent of students who felt their parents were happily married and still in love believed they maintained this happy state without the help of sex, or at least not much of it."

Some students reacted very negatively, apparently not wanting to even think about their parents' sex life: " 'This questionnaire stinks.' 'Whoever thinks about their parents' sexual relations, except perverts?' 'What stupid . . . person made up these questions?' "[1]

Men in mid-life tend to carry the same convictions as the college students regarding sex after forty. They believe that sex is over by mid-life, so when they first experience some sexual slowness, they react with trauma and believe they are now too old for sex.

SEXUAL EXPECTATIONS

Much of the problem with the sex life of a man at mid-life is that his expectations are not based on reality. For example, a man who was a pole vaulter in college and cleared 16′ 2″ does not expect at age forty-five to match the performance. Yet, when he thinks of his sex life, he anticipates that his recycling speed will be the same as when he was a young adult.

The male in his late teens is at the very peak of his sexual capacity. He achieves an erection very rapidly and can experience a number of ejaculations with only a few minutes' recovery time. From the late teens and early twenties there is a very slow loss of recovery speed throughout the rest of his life. A man in good health in his seventies, however, still should have no problem having sexual intercourse, although it will take more time to achieve an erection and more time until ejaculation.

It is a mistake for a man in his forties to expect the same kind of sexual capacity as the adolescent or young adult. However, a man at forty, while his sexual pace is somewhat slower, is by far a more effective lover. He understands more completely the needs of his wife and his slower pace until ejaculation makes the sexual relationship more fulfilling.

Some mid-life men have been trapped by the office or locker room escapades. They feel that to prove they have macho, they must match the performance of the adolescent boy. Women, however, are not looking for a sexual performance like that of the adolescent boy, but of the mature man who understands love, warmth, and caring.

SEXUAL PROBLEMS

The loss of sexual ability is most often due to fear rather than physical causes. Some men have become fathers very late in life. "A South African called Henry Potts and a Pole named Kasper Raynold became fathers at the age of 105. It's said that a Frenchman, Pierre Deformel, fathered children in three centuries, the birth dates being 1699, 1738 and 1801."[2]

Sometimes a man worries that he may lose his capacity if he has a heart attack. "According to Drs. Ernest Friedman and Herman Hellerstein of Case Western Reserve University, the pulse rate [during sexual intercourse] does not rise more than it does during many other routine activities, and the period of maximum acceleration usually lasts only about fifteen seconds; they conclude that 'over 80 percent of men (and presumably women) who have had coronaries can fulfill the demands of sexual activity without evidence of significant strain.' "[3]

An increasing number of men in mid-life are showing up in the general practitioner's office, complaining that they are impotent; yet most impotence is really emotionally based. Quite often the man who claims to be impotent can have sexual intercourse while he is on vacation or may be sexually aroused at a movie. Fear is the basis of sexual problems.

The correction of sexual problems must be seen from more than a physical point of view, as shown by a number of studies and experiments using hormone therapy. Sheehy reports on a study in which fifty men complaining of impotence were given hormone tablets and another fifty complaining of impotence were given sugar pills. Seventy-eight percent on the hormone tablets improved their sexual capacity after a month, and 40 percent on the sugar pills improved.[4]

Masters and Johnson list six general conditions that cause the aging male to lose sexual responsiveness:

1. Monotony of a repetitious relationship.
2. Preoccupation with career or economic pursuits.

3. Mental or physical fatigue.
4. Overindulgence in food or drink.
5. Physical and mental infirmities of a man or his spouse.
6. Fear of failure in the sex act.[5]

It's important to notice that emotions play the major part in the loss of sexual ability. If a man is going through stress at work so that his self-image is being diminished, he likely will have a lessening of sexual responsiveness.

Stanley Frank reports what happened to men sexually when the stock market crashed in 1929: "Six months later, it was routine to hear women say that they had had no sexual relations with their husbands since Black Thursday, the day the bottom fell out of the market."[6]

Without question there is a slight slowing down of the sexual response of the man in mid-life. This slowing down is not negative but, in fact, should make his sexual relationships with his wife richer and more pleasurable. When there is a loss of sexual capacity in mid-life, the high probability is that it has little to do with medical causes and relates more to some other cause, such as a low self-image, fatigue, overextension at work, or too much alcohol. Fear that he will lose his sexual capacity will, in fact, cause him to lose it.

Not all sexual problems at mid-life are from emotional stress, however. A number of studies show that a hormonal imbalance can develop in men at mid-life, similar to some of the hormonal changes women experience. This sometimes causes morning fatigue, depression, nervousness, difficulty with sleeping, sometimes affecting the heartbeat and also sexual potency to some degree. This hormonal imbalance also strongly affects the man's emotional life. He seems to lose stability, becomes easily irritated at work and at home, and may have wildly vascillating moods.

IMPROVING HIS SEX LIFE

It's a mistake for a man to think that the answer to his sexual problems lies in some new techniques. The basic way to improve sexual relationships is to practice sex with love. "The real issue, of course, isn't making love; it's *feeling loved*."[7] Or, as Frank puts it, "A man is never more alone than when he is locked in a loveless sexual embrace."[8]

If a man is going to improve his sex life, he must shift his attention away from himself and begin to concentrate on his wife and her needs. As the emphasis shifts from performance to caring, the relationship will improve in quality, and performance will probably also improve.

Sexual therapists Masters and Johnson, when trying to help a couple reestablish sexual relationships, concentrate on trying to build the emotional relationship before the physical relationship. The couple agrees *not* to have sexual intercourse until it is eagerly sought by both of them, so the concentration is shifted to building the relationship through sharing common interests, talking, and touching each other. The emphasis is always on the relationship, not on sexual intercourse. These therapists have found that when the pressure for sexual performance is removed and the emphasis is shifted toward the relationship, sexual interest returns to the couple.

A man's religious convictions may have to change to bring about an improvement in his sex life. Many Christians still believe that the original sin in the Garden of Eden was that Adam and Eve had sexual intercourse. That's ridiculous! The original sin was disobeying God and eating a piece of fruit from a forbidden tree.

Before the act of disobedience, God instructed Adam and Eve to "multiply and fill the earth and subdue it" (Gen. 1:28). Somehow many people believe that God was stunned when he came into the garden one evening and discovered that Adam and Eve had intercourse. Sex is not a surprise to God; he planned for it. He intended that couples should have a sexual relationship. One of the purposes of sex is for procreation, that is, to have children.

Procreation is not the only purpose, however. The Bible clearly teaches that there is also a recreational aspect to sex. The Scripture reveals that the woman's physical body is to be enjoyed all the time by her husband. "Let your fountain be blessed, and rejoice in the wife of your youth. As a loving hind and a graceful doe, let her breasts satisfy you at all times; be exhilarated always with her love" (Prov. 5:18-19, NASB). Sex is not only for bringing children into the world. The man is to be intoxicated with his wife's love all the time.

The Song of Solomon is a celebration of love, expressing how the young man feels toward his love. He talks about her eyes, hair, teeth; he speaks of her lips, mouth, neck, and also the beauty of her breasts. He declares, "You are altogether beautiful, my darling, and there is no blemish in you" (4:7, NASB).

Some people have tried to make this an allegory of God's love for us. Certainly it can be used to show that, but the primary purpose is to show the physical love relationship between a husband and his wife.

The New Testament gives instructions about a husband and wife having sexual relationships: "So do not refuse these rights to each other. The only exception to this rule would be the agreement of both husband and wife to refrain from the rights of marriage for a limited time, so that they can give themselves more completely to prayer. Afterwards, they should come together again so that Satan won't be able to tempt them because of their lack of self-control" (I Cor. 7:5). The Bible is clearly teaching that sex has a recreational aspect, that is, that the couple should experience sex regularly and refrain from sex *only* as they mutually agree to spend their time in prayer. After prayer, they are to engage in sex again.

The Bible teaches that sex is procreational and recreational, and this passage also points out that sex is *relational*. The husband and the wife agree on when to have sex and when not to. There is a clear relationship established between them, where they are both making decisions about the sex act. It is *not* a male-dominated or an animal act but rather a sexual experience involving both husband and wife who mutually love and respect each other and who are sensitively communicating with each other.

When couples come to me seeking help with sexual problems, we generally start by looking at their emotional relationship. Eighty to ninety percent of sexual problems can be cured by helping the couple reduce tension between each other and relate positively on an emotional basis.

After we have worked through the emotional differences, some simple teaching and hints often help the sexual relationship to improve. I am grateful to see a number of writers who have a deep confidence in God and who also trust the Scriptures writing more explicitly about the sexual relationship between married couples. There are a number of good books and tapes available at Christian bookstores that can help a man in mid-life with his sexual life.

WE'RE DIFFERENT

A common element that many couples don't understand is the different excitement levels of the male and the female. Most men are aroused very rapidly and reach the point of ejaculation quickly. Then they are ready to roll over and go to sleep.

The husband's excitement rate can be likened to the heat of a gas burner—quickly on and quickly off—while the wife is more like an electric burner—slowly on and slowly off.

When a husband and wife don't understand their excitement differences, they begin to think that the other is taking advantage of them. The wife feels the husband simply wants to satisfy himself and doesn't care about her; she feels used. The husband, on the other hand, feels his wife is frigid and unresponsive. If the husband understands this difference and slows down his excitement rate, he can give his wife time to catch up so that together they can reach a peak of excitement and enjoyment at the same moment. If a couple will spend more time in foreplay, arousing each other before the act of intercourse, they will be more likely to arrive at a climax at the same time.

It is also important for the husband to realize that his wife is slow in coming down from a sexual high. If he rolls over and goes to sleep, she is more likely to feel used. The coming-down time is a good time to talk, to tell each other how much they appreciate each other, to thank each other—not only for sex but for the little things they do for each other. The coming-down time is a good time to make plans for what they want to do as a couple, things they'd like to achieve. Some men feel that the coming-down time is a waste; they'd rather go to sleep. But if the wife continues to fondle her husband and he continues to touch and caress his wife, the coming-down time can be a rich period for building the marital relationship.

WHAT TURNS YOU ON?

A couple needs to tell each other specifically what gives them the most pleasure—how they liked to be touched, what position they like the best; in short, what causes the greatest sexual satisfaction. Many couples have never shared with each other the things that cause sexual pleasure. Sometimes they are too embarrassed, or they are afraid that their partner will feel bad if they bring this up. Most sexual relationships could be improved if the couple would share these simple facts.

VARIETY IS THE SPICE OF SEX

A couple told me in a counseling session about their growing disillusionment with sex. It had lost its sparkle and excitement. Before they were married, they could hardly keep their hands off each other, but now it was "just plain Dullsville." I encouraged them to think back to their courtship days and remember the kinds of things that aroused them. I challenged them to break out of the mold of having sexual intercourse late at night just before they went to sleep. That time is probably most typical, but from an energy point of view, it is the worst choice.

Why not go for a drive in the country and have sex there? How about sex over the lunch hour? Why not on the living room floor in front of the fireplace? What's wrong with sex in a canoe?

One doctor tells of an older couple who had tapered off to having intercourse every four weeks or so. Then the wife became ill and they had no relations for about six months. When she tried to resume intercourse, the husband could not get an erection. So the wife went out and bought a book on sex, and read that if a wife fondled her husband's penis it helped him have an erection. One might think that this is common knowledge, but she had been taught that playing with sex organs was not something a decent woman did. She bravely tried it anyway and it worked. In fact she experienced their lovemaking as far better than thirty years ago, and her husband as a changed man, cheerful, optimistic, and vigorous. The wife then remarked, "Maybe I shouldn't admit it but I enjoy our relations more than I used to. I'm even thinking of trying some of the other things I read about in that book."⁹

Sexual intercourse is an experience a couple can enjoy repeatedly, and each time it can be new, full, and complete. One time it may take on a very serious tone with deep, interpersonal sharing. Another time it might be just plain fun. Dr. David Reuben, author of *Everything You Always Wanted to Know About Sex But Were Afraid to Ask*, says with tongue in cheek that "one act of intercourse is equal to half an hour of jogging, and that 'once around the bed' is the exercise equivalent of running four times around the park."¹⁰

It's time that people realize that sex is God's idea, that he intends it to be a pleasurable experience, enjoyed frequently by a husband and wife. When a man and a woman accept the biblical basis for sex, work on their emotional relationship, and seek to learn all they can about each other and a meaningful sexual relationship, then they will have overcome one of the major problem-causing areas in the mid-life crisis.

> Thank you for making me so wonderfully complex! It is amazing to think about. Your workmanship is marvelous—and how well I know it. (Ps. 139:14)

20
WORK THAT'S FUN

THE SECOND MAJOR CONCERN a man must face, if he is to successfully make it through the mid-life crisis, is his attitude and involvement with work. Marriage and sex will be the most significant areas for a man emotionally, but the problem of work will probably consume more of his time. He can't avoid facing the work crisis that comes in mid-life. Copping out by early retirement is not a long-range solution. It only delays the inevitable question, "What kind of contribution do I want to make to society that will, at the same time, enable me to earn a living?"

When a man started out on the ladder of success, he seemed to find only upward progress through his twenties and thirties and into the forties. As he succeeded in his job, his job expanded in responsibility. It was an inverted pyramid—the job started out small, but as he rose toward success, he moved both upward and out-ward.

As the job expanded, more people wanted it. Competi-tion became stronger. By the time he reaches his mid-forties, he is possibly overextended. At the same time, his physical energies are beginning to level off.

As soon as the man begins to recognize that he cannot continuously expand in his job because of his limited energy, he often begins to feel insecure. His self-image may be damaged, and he may feel that he is trapped because he cannot slow down due to financial pressures, trapped because the people in the company want him to keep advancing, and trapped because there are younger competitors wanting his job. If he shows weakness, he may be replaced.

Or, he may be in a situation such as this: "A worker approaching forty, after making steady progress for al-most two decades, suddenly finds himself on a plateau with no further prospect of advancement. Shall he give up the security he has earned over the years and take a chance in a job with another company? Or shall he whit-tle down his ambitions to fit his circumstances?"[1]

Another change comes to a man in his mid-forties. He is now expected to shift from being a competitor with other men to being their trainer. Up to this point, he has been working himself up in the company, trying always to do something better than others so he can be recog-nized and advanced. He progressed by competition from stockroom boy to loading dock, to foreman, to vice-president in charge of shipping. Now the company asks him to change his direction and begin to train the younger men under him, to work with the stock boy, the foreman, and to pick out key men in the company and train them for advancement.

It is never said aloud, but the vice-president knows that what he really is being asked to do is to train someone to take his job. This requires a totally different mindset. He is no longer in competition with men beneath him; now he is to equip them to eventually take his position. At this time in life there is a deep and pervading reality of the man's own mortality and ultimate death. Suddenly he has passed over a line. "A vague feeling dawns on one that not only machines but people—especially middle-aged people—become obsolescent."[2]

HIS ATTITUDES TOWARD WORK

A man has to resist the temptation to run, to get away, to retreat into self-pity, to react in anger and cynicism. He has to go back to basics: What is it all about? Why do we work in the first place? *Leben und arbeiten* ("to love and to work"), said Freud, is the need of every man. If he hasn't found fulfillment here, he hasn't reached maturity.

"Work supplies an answer to some of the deepest and most basic of all human drives: the need to produce something, the need to create something, the need to gratify curiosity, the need to be useful, the need to be needed. Wise men have always known this. 'Blessed is he who has found his work,' wrote Thomas Carlyle."[3]

There is a basic, built-in need for men to work. Work is not a violation of man; it is, rather, an important ingredient to fulfill man. Some people believe that work was part of the curse God placed on man because of sin, but it is important to realize that work was present before the Fall of man: "And God blessed them and told them, 'Multiply and fill the earth and subdue it; you are masters of the fish and birds and all the animals' " (Gen. 1:28).

The directive here is to master the earth, to be rulers over it. The Bible continues, "The Lord God placed the man in the Garden of Eden as its gardener, to tend and care for it" (Gen. 2:15). Here God is giving man the responsibility of work.

Before the Fall, man was given the responsibility of administration and oversight, that is, management, as well as the physical activity of tending the garden. We see two dimensions of work here—one of a laborer and the other of a manager. Work is part of the plan of God to minister to the nature of man.

It's important for a man to see that God is involved in his work as well as in every other dimension of life. More than that, it is important for him to realize that as he gives his life to God, God will form interests and desires within his personality that should then be expressed through work. "For God is at work within you, helping you want to obey him, and then helping you do what he wants" (Phil. 2:13). God places desires within a man's personality; then he gives a man the capacity to carry out those desires. It is completely appropriate for a man to ask God's direction in his work life. It is absolutely right for a man to look within himself and ask what his interests are. Finding the right job is matching our God-given interests and abilities with various occupational opportunities.

Over the years I have noticed a number of men caught in unhappy work situations. When I was in college, my father told me that no one really enjoyed work, but it was something everyone had to do to live. At that time he was in the heating and air conditioning business. When he got into his mid-sixties, he felt God wanted him to start a retirement village in Florida. Dad works as many hours as he used to in the old business, but now what he is doing seems to have greater purpose. His God-given desires and abilities have beautifully meshed so that out of a pastureland in central Florida has sprung up not only a retirement village but an expression of a man who has found that work, even though tiring, can be very exhilarating.

THE WORKAHOLIC

There are three major ways a man reacts to the work crisis at mid-life. He may push harder than ever to try to demonstrate that he is valuable. Or he may feel discouraged, exploited, or sick of the rat race, and decide to completely drop out. Or he may change jobs, sometimes entering a very different occupation, and find more fulfillment in his work than he has ever known.

"The present generation of middle-agers has, for the most part, been raised on the pablum of the work ethic. Admit it or not, that is our hang-up. We have measured our worth by our work."[4] If a man measures his worth by his work, he will be frustrated at the peak of mid-life when he no longer has the energy for increased responsibility in his job.

If a man chooses to work harder, he will find that to be a dead-end road. The man who becomes a workaholic to prove himself is only delaying the inevitable—sooner or later he must face himself and make some realistic evaluations of his capacities and strengths. His physical body will not allow him to work forever at an expanding level.

I tend to be one of those workaholics, and in recent months I have found it necessary to say to myself, "Your energy and strength are limited. Now choose to spend those in the way you can be most productive." The problem I have with my job is that I enjoy doing so many different things. I now must choose to do the ones that will be the most helpful to the church and the most satisfying to me.

THE DREAM HAS GONE DRY

Another direction a man may take is to give up, to become disillusioned with his job—"What's it all worth anyway? I've broken my back for this company all these years, and now they're just going to push me aside."

As an expression of this, a man's productivity at work will show a downturn. Dr. Jermyn McCahan, chief medical director of AT & T Long Lines, said on a television show in June, 1974,

> Our company has begun to recognize that there is such a thing as middle-age crisis, which can occur usually between the ages of thirty-five and fifty and usually manifests itself by an individual changing in his style of behavior and in his productivity. We detect these symptoms in our people usually when a supervisor contacts us and indicates that an employee is beginning to slip, and he may tell us that their absence record or attendance record is beginning to become a problem, their productivity, either in quality or quantity is becoming an issue. . . .[5]

As a man becomes less productive, he is really expressing passive resistance to his job. He is quietly waving a red flag. In a sense, he is saying, "Please fire me or move me to another job. I don't like what I'm doing, but I don't have the courage to get out without someone pushing me."

In the life of the church, where many volunteers are

225

involved, we often see this passive resistance and dis-satisfaction. The best solution is to talk frankly with the person and place him in a responsibility that more adequately fits his abilities and interests.

Instead of dropping out or slowing down, a man needs to face the reasons for his job dissatisfaction and bring about the necessary changes.

HE HATES HIS JOB

Another common way of expressing dissatisfaction with a job is anger. A man may become extremely cynical of work itself and of his job in particular. He will probably also be difficult to live with at work. He will be short-tempered and critical, walking around with a chip on his shoulder. Young associates may receive the greatest mistreatment, especially if he sees them as competitors for his job. His anger may also verge on insubordination to his bosses if he feels the business is not going the way it ought to go and that he is really wasting his life working for this company.

Dale Tarnowieski, in a survey entitled *The Changing Success Ethic*, says, "An alarming 40 percent of all surveyed middle managers and 52 percent of the reporting supervisory managers say they find their work, at best, unsatisfying."[6] There are many reasons why a man may consider his job unsatisfying, but most of these reasons come down to one central cause—a man's interest, values, goals, and abilities in his life do not match what he is doing in his job. The closer a person can come to matching his entire personality and life-style with a job, the greater degree of satisfaction he can expect.

Often in mid-life we hear people suggesting to men

that they slow down, take it easy, and sometimes the man in mid-life decides this is the solution for his job frustrations. It is not that the man is incapable of handling the job; it is rather that there is a *mismatch* of the man, including his goals and personality as well as his abilities, with his job.

Why can a man work nine hours at the office and come home absolutely drained and worn out with emotional frustration, then over the weekend take a bunch of Boy Scouts through the trauma of camping out and come back exhausted but not emotionally fatigued?

Escaping from work is not the answer. The answer is a better alignment of the man with his job.

If a man is following a normal growth pattern, we can assume that he will outgrow a series of jobs; that is, he will find these jobs not challenging—not in line with his personality at his state of growth. Emotional gaps will develop as the man grows personally while his job stays the same.

One summer in Cleveland during my college years, I worked in a machine shop. I ran several different machines, but I quickly learned that none of them demanded *all* of me. A highly trained gorilla could have carried out my tasks. My job was to punch a button to start the machine, dump a pan of bolts in one end of the machine, wait for a pan to fill up at the other end of the machine, and remove it. To keep from going insane, I wrote letters and memorized large sections of the Bible.

HOPEFUL, YET AFRAID

The same pressures that cause a man to become a workaholic, or to be disillusioned and want to drop out, can be the springboard toward an exciting new work alignment in his life.

A person standing on the outside and looking in might quickly suggest an intensive evaluation process followed by career changes to fit his personality and abilities. The man in mid-life probably will not go through that process, however, because he is afraid. He is afraid to find out about himself. That may make him more unhappy with his job, and he is afraid to do anything that would risk losing his job. He hopes that somehow this frustration with work will simply disappear. One man put it this way. "I'm fifty-four years old. Fifteen years ago, if they had told me, 'Listen, we can't give you a raise,' I might have said, '. . . You can take this job and. . . ,' and I would have gone somewhere else. But when it happened now, where could I go? Who is hiring fifty-four-year-old men these days?"[7]

Another man said,

I am fifty-two years old now, and I became a vice-president when I was forty-four. That was considered quite young at the time. I felt very successful and secure. Two weeks ago a twenty-seven year old kid became a vice-president of the firm! He's sharp and bright and "with it." He speaks in the idiom of the young; he brings with him all the contemporary thinking of his college professors. The top executives are aware of how rapidly the world is changing, and they know that to be successful they have to be contemporary and able to change. I agree, but I get a hollow feeling of terror in the pit of my stomach; if vice-presidents are made at twenty-seven, when am I going to be obsolete?[8]

Arthur Miller's play *Death of a Salesman* is a tragic commentary on our society's ability to throw away people. It is the truth of this play that causes many men in mid-life to live not only in fear but in *stark terror* of losing their jobs. Willy Loman, a shoe salesman, is in his sixties. He is a broken, worn-out man who has traded his energy in life for the benefit of the company. He asks for an easier job but is fired instead. Willy's response is, "I put thirty-four years into this firm, Howard, and now I can't pay my insurance. You can't eat the orange and throw the peel away—a man is not a piece of fruit."[9]

Many a wife does not fully grasp the intensity of the terror her husband feels regarding work. He has always come across strong and secure. He has always seemed to know where he was going. Unfortunately, to him his job is an expression of his worth, and if he loses his job, he has lost his worth. "When an insecure husband asks, 'What will I do if I lose my job?' his wife mentally responds, 'Get another.' But the fear-inhibited man, with far less confidence in his abilities than his spouse, inevitably retorts, 'Where?' "[10]

The stress produced by a man's unhappiness with his work and the fear of losing his job will cause a number of physical and emotional effects such as ulcers, high blood pressure, colitis, impotence, and nervous breakdown.

HE LOSES HIS JOB

The only thing more devastating to a man than being dissatisfied with his job or being afraid of losing it is actually losing it. When a man loses his salary, he also loses the benefits—family hospitalization plans, retirement benefits that quite often cannot be transferred to any other job, paid vacations, sick leave, and use of company recreational facilities. He may also lose items such as a car, expense accounts, or other fringe benefits.

There is, however, a greater loss than either the salary

or additional benefits. When he loses his job, he loses his self-identity. He feels like a nothing. It's difficult to meet people, because most conversation centers around what you do as an identification of who you are. A man then tends to retreat and draw back into a hole.

When I graduated from seminary in 1957, I went for the next eight months without being called to a church. There were a number of opportunities, but I did not feel that any of them was the place God wanted me to be. In 1969, I was three months between churches. During both of these periods in my life, there was a tremendous loss of self-esteem. I felt as if no one really wanted me or my services; I felt useless; I was convinced that God didn't care for me; I didn't want to be with people; I was embarrassed to talk about the situation with my children; in short, I felt extremely wretched.

During both of these times I was employed, but not at a job that used my gifts, abilities, and my calling from God. Repeatedly, during these times Sally would encourage me that I still was a minister, even though I was not, at that time, actively ministering in a church.

JOB DISCRIMINATION

In 1967 Congress passed an age discrimination act, which is administered by the Employment Standards Administration of the Department of Labor. This law forbids discrimination against people between ages forty and sixty-five on the basis of age. "Since 1968, many thousands of complaints for age discrimination have been dealt with by the E.S.A.; in fiscal 1973 alone, for instance, the agency took more than 7,000 investigative actions, found age discrimination in over a third of these cases, and got compliance in nearly all of them."[11]

This legal action should go a long way toward reducing the fear that a man has about losing his job. He can no longer be pushed out the door simply because he is over forty. Thousands of companies and jobs are being changed by this new legal action. "In fiscal 1973 alone, E.S.A. actions opened up nearly 40,000 job opportunities of various sorts that have been illegally age-restricted, and an unknown but surely vast number of other job opportunities were opened up by employers who voluntarily complied with the law without having to be forced to do so."[12]

The Inner World of the Middle-Aged Man has an extensive section on job discrimination, which may serve as a helpful resource to a man struggling with this problem.

Our local newspaper carried an article entitled "Court Rules in Favor of Jet Pilot, 58." It's the story of Phillip Houghton, who was grounded by the McDonnell-Douglas Corporation because, they said, he was too old to be a test pilot. The only basis for that grounding was Houghton's age. Houghton filed suit in January, 1973, against the company, and the Labor Department took up the challenge. After an extensive court battle, the Supreme Court on November 28, 1977, ordered McDonnell-Douglas to pay Houghton six years in back pay, estimated at about $200,000. The court "agreed with Houghton, finding no statistics to back the company's contention that test pilots in their 50s are less effective than younger co-workers."[13]

CHANGING CAREERS

Gone are the days for most men when they can choose

a career in their adolescent years and follow that job completely through their lives. Second, third, and even fourth careers are not at all abnormal these days, because of rapid technological changes and the knowledge explosion. It is important for a man not to view himself as failing if he changes careers, but rather he should think of himself as more successful to move to a career or job that more adequately fits him. "Most persons working at sixty-five moved on from their previous jobs in their middle forties, and we suspect that this was caused less by economic factors than by middle-age discontent."[14] It is unfortunate for a man to stay in a job or career that no longer challenges him nor matches his life.

A man may choose a new career very similar to his old job, or he may choose one that is very different. Smith, in his book *49 and Holding*, speaks of ministers who left the ministry in mid-life: "It would be impossible to list all of the kinds of occupations which have been chosen. Here is a sample: college teaching, high school counseling, real estate, county health, county welfare, juvenile parole officer, insurance, personnel, business management, banking, golf pro, school administration. The opportunities are related to skills and training."[15]

The new career or job will not be successful nor meaningful simply because it is a change. It must be a change that puts a man's working energies in line with his gifts, abilities, and values in life.

Large sections of the book *New Life Begins at Forty* by Peterson speak of the career changes men and women have made at mid-life. For example, Charles Darrow at age forty-five lost his job as a stove salesman and then invented the game Monopoly, which earned him more than a million dollars. Wallace Johnson was broke at age forty, decided to go into business, borrowed money to build a house, and later became one of the cofounders of

Holiday Inn. Walter Knott was in his forties when he decided to start selling boysenberries. This venture later became the famous Knott's Berry Farm. The Jack Nagles of Streator, Illinois, owned a dry-cleaning business. They wanted more free time, so they sold that business and bought a drive-in restaurant. They now work hard for six months and have six months of vacation. Peterson records incident after incident of people who evaluated their lives, their interests and abilities, and then changed their jobs to fit that new interest and life-style.[16]

A career change may not mean moving to a totally different job or even to a different company. It may mean a sideways move that does not increase the responsibility or the work load but fits the man's personality more completely.

Sometimes the sideward movement of a man will be from one company to another. For example, John DeLorean of General Motors resigned a $550,000-a-year corporate vice-presidency to start his own company. DeLorean was the creator of the Firebird. He felt that General Motors was too conservative and not really in touch with the needs of people or the energy problems. His dream is to build a safe sports car that "will enable drivers to survive accidents at closing speeds as high as 100 miles per hour, and have twice the fuel economy of a Chevrolet Corvette."[17]

HOW TO CHANGE JOBS

The temptation that a man must strongly resist is to take *any* job that comes along. The problem is not only unemployment but also one of being wrongly employed. A man came to my office a couple of years ago, wanting my advice about a job. At that time he was earning in the $20,000 range. He had a job offer starting at $30,000, with promises of a salary raise to $40,000 in a couple years. I asked him why he was attracted to the job. His first answer was the money.

When I asked what other reasons he had for liking the job, the answers came more slowly and seemed forced. I then asked him to list the reasons he did not like the job. Those responses flowed freely and in great abundance. We had talked only a few minutes before he came to realize that simply taking another job would not solve his problem, even if it had an attractive salary attached to it. As a result, he did not take the job but went into business for himself.

Perhaps the best book available today about career change is *What Color Is Your Parachute?* by Richard N. Bolles. This is a tough, no-fooling-around book that deals with the problem of unemployment and under-employment. It is a self-study that will involve a great deal of a man's time. Bolles points out that a man in mid-life may have anywhere from 20,000 to 60,000 hours of working time ahead, and "you're automatically talking about $150,000-500,000 of potential income."[18] Bolles's purpose is not simply to help people find another job but to help them find the right job that matches their God-given abilities.

He offers three keys:

Key No. 1: You must decide just exactly what you want to do.

Key No. 2: You must decide just exactly where you want to do it, through your own research and personal survey.

Key No. 3: You must research the organizations that interest you at great length, and then approach the one individual in each organization who has the power to hire you for the job that you have decided you want to do.[19]

This self-help book leads a man through an evaluation of his goals, an inventory of his skills, the establishment of time goals, and the development of his job self-confidence.

Bolles makes no apology for the extensive time involvement that a man will make in the process of finding the right career and the right job. He says, "It is worth spending two weeks of your life, or two months, or whatever it takes to plan well—so that what you do those 20 or 30 thousand hours is something you enjoy and something you do well and something that fits in with your life mission."[20]

CAREER COUNSELING MAY HELP

Richard Bolles and John Crystal have coauthored a book entitled *Where Do I Go from Here with My Life?* Crystal heads up his own organization called Crystal Management Services, Inc., which is not an employment agency but a career counseling firm that helps a man understand who he is and what his potentials are. As he leads a man through the process of self-evaluation, the result is a positive self-image, which enables this man to go out and sell himself to a potential employer. (This type of agency can be found in most major population centers of the United States.)

Crystal and Bolles emphatically warn the job hunter not to depend on employment agencies to find a job for him. They point out, "Some big corporations receive as many as 250,000 resumes a year. . . . The Federal Trade Commission has reported the success rate of private employment agencies as about 5 percent."[21]

Finding a job or moving into a new career will finally

come down to knowing yourself—including your life-style, values, strengths, and abilities—and then by research discovering the type of place where you'd like to live and the kind of company you'd like to work for. The third stage is then to make yourself invaluable to that company and available to the one person who can hire you.

WORK SELF-IMAGE

The battle of employment is going to be won or lost in a man's mind, in the way he thinks of himself. He must realize he is worthwhile and, in fact, crucial to the functioning of our society. People in mid-life are in command. The whole of society hinges on the ability of people in mid-life to continue contributing.

It's important for a man also to realize that he has distinct employment advantages over other ages. Hunt in *Prime Time* points out several of these advantages:

Non-disabling injuries on the job are highest among 20- to 29-year-olds, and decline for each age group thereafter, reaching their lowest levels for workers in the 70 to 74 category.

. . . Older workers have lower absentee rates than younger ones, despite the generally better health of the young. . . .

A study of 6,000 federal mail sorters, for example, revealed that persons 45 to 49 sorted more consistently than those 35 to 44, and those 50 to 54 did still better; the 55 to 59 group dropped off a trifle (but was still above the 35 to 44 level), while the highest consistency level of all was that of sorters 60 and over.

. . . Older workers in the steel mill and various light-industry plants were generally as productive as younger men, while those in retailing, clerical, and managerial work were actually more productive than their younger co-workers.[22]

It is encouraging to know that men and women in mid-life have the lowest unemployment rate. Figures from the Bureau of Labor Statistics show that, rather than being discarded by society, people in mid-life seem to be more eagerly sought.

1976 Unemployment Percentage Rates[23]

Age	Male	Female
16-19	19.2	18.7
20-24	12.0	11.9
25-34	6.2	8.5
35-44	4.1	6.1
45-54	4.0	5.2
55-64	4.2	4.9

One scholar evaluated the lives of 738 creative people, then categorized their output in each age of their lives by percentage. His studies show that the overall productivity of their lives came not in early adulthood but in mid-life.

HIS WIFE CAN HELP

If a man has a good relationship with his wife, and she is willing to stand by him through it all, his self-image and confidence will be improved. He will have the courage to consider a job that might be more closely aligned with who he is at this age in life. Women were asked the question, " 'If your husband were to tell you he hated his work and wanted to quit and either go back to school or get a job with much less pay, how would you feel? What would you do?' The majority of women gave this kind of answer: 'I guess I'd be scared at first—I would worry—but I would never say, "No." I'd be willing to change our way of living—and after the first shock, I think part of me would be relieved and glad.' "[24] Quite often the process of considering a career change will draw a husband and wife closer together, perhaps in the sense of the two of them against the world.

TAKE HOPE! GOD IS AT WORK

A major factor in improving a man's work self-image may be the activity of God deep within his personality. If a man believes that God is his friend and wants the best for him, he'll be able to trust this uncertain process of work relocation into God's hands. That doesn't in any way infer that the man becomes passive or inactive. Instead he is deeply aware of a divine umbrella of protection. God, who has made everything, will control his thoughts and at the same time open doors of opportunity that really fit his life.

Many sections in the Bible have personally encouraged me about the future. For example, Psalm 37:23-26. This doesn't promise that I will not have struggles in my life, but it promises that my struggles won't destroy me. It promises that God will not forsake me, not because I am so good, but because he loves me. Further, it promises that God will bless me so I can be a blessing to other people, and that the blessing and impact of God in my life will not end with my life but will continue in the lives of my children.

Sometimes people say to me, "I know God loves me. I know he wants the best for me. I can see he is giving me special gifts and abilities. But how do I know that an employer will want me?"

Proverbs 21:1 says, "Just as water is turned into irrigation ditches, so the Lord directs the king's thoughts. He turns them wherever he wants to." God is not only at work in your life, but he is also at work in the lives of other people who will be involved in your employment process. God is going to fit all the pieces of the puzzle together for the full utilization and development of your life.

A deep confidence in God will not make a man inactive but rather will arouse his expectation and fuel the search to find the place God has for him.

Peterson gives some good historic perspective to the problem of unemployment and the search for relocation: "Our nation wasn't built by men and women who got off the boat in New York, Boston, or Baltimore and waited for someone to employ them. If they couldn't find work in harbor cities they went hunting for opportunities where they could find them. They learned a new language. They acquired new knowledge and understanding. And they demonstrated a willingness to master new skills and go where the jobs were. This pioneer philosophy should guide mature job seekers today."[25]

As a man frankly faces his job situation, his own personality, his interests, and his God-given abilities, and as he seeks to make job or career changes that fit him, he will begin to find a resolution to another area of his mid-life crisis. Each time he resolves a major concern in his life, he will notice the other areas will also improve. It isn't important to tackle all of the areas at once, but it is important to face the major concerns of mid-life and, one by one, resolve them. As each one is resolved, it will give him increased strength to resolve others.

> I stand silently before the Lord, waiting for him to rescue me. For salvation comes from him alone. Yes, he alone is my Rock, my rescuer, defense and fortress. Why then should I be tense with fear when troubles come? (Ps. 62:1-2)

21
AGING WITH FINESSE

THERE IS NO WAY OF SIDESTEPPING the aging process. A man in his forties *is* getting older. There aren't any creams or special injections or fountains of youth that will stop the process. It is true that his mental and physical processes are aging, but more important is how old he sees himself. Some men are very old at thirty-five because they have lost the reason for living and they feel they have nothing more to contribute to life; other men continue to be extremely productive because they believe they have a contribution to make.

The trick in aging is to be both realistic and optimistic. Will a man give up as he sees the first gray hairs and wrinkles, or will he structure his energies in ways that will cause him to continue to be valuable?

A man may have always felt that "old is bad." Then

mid-life comes, and he has a mental image of shriveled, helpless old men, rocking endlessly and uselessly on the porch of the local nursing home. This vision is not based on reality but on his own self-image and fears about the future.

FACTS ABOUT MENTAL AGING

Studies show a different story than this. "In one study, for instance, a group of college freshmen were tested with the Army Alpha intelligence test, and forty-two years later those who were still alive were given the same test—and showed an increase in scores.... Psychologist K. Warner Schaie of the University of Southern California completed a major longitudinal study which showed that distinct increases take place in various dimensions of intelligence during middle age...."[1]

Spontaneous, unique creativity tends to come earlier in life, while creativity that requires the absorption of wisdom tends to come later. There is no basis in fact to say that the mental aging process causes a person to lose overall creativity.

The question is, can older people learn new tricks? Yes, the studies show that they can. They might not learn them as quickly. But the greater problem is they're not so easily convinced that they need to learn new tricks. It isn't the ability they've lost, but the desire and the pace.

People in mid-life commonly complain of their forgetfulness, although studies show that there is little long-term memory loss. What bothers most people is the business of misplacing things, setting something down and not remembering five minutes later where they put it. This, however, seems to have nothing to do with a man's brain cells; it is more likely related to what he thinks he can do. "It has been estimated that as few as 10 percent of our brain cells disappear even over a long lifetime. It is only the *fear* that you are too old to learn new tricks that limits you, not any shortage of cerebral capacity."[2]

PHYSICAL AGING

A man in mid-life will, no doubt, notice physical aging more than mental aging. He is constantly confronted with his mirror when he shaves.

If he finds his self-worth tied to his physical abilities, he is likely to experience a great deal of self-image loss during mid-life. Men, such as athletes, who are highly oriented toward their physical prowess and have a high physical identity, can become old in their early thirties. On the other hand, a teacher or a salesman who does not gain his self-image from his physical performance may not be old until he is in his seventies or eighties.

What is the aging process for a man in mid-life? He loses physical strength, but this should be compensated for by his increased experience.

The recuperative powers of the man in mid-life are also reduced. "At twenty, you can stay out until 3:00 A.M. and still be in at the office at 9:00 without the boss or you knowing the difference; but in middle age, if you are out after midnight, it may take a day or two to regain normal efficiency. The skin wound that heals on a twenty-year-old in seven days heals for a forty-year-old in fourteen days."[3]

The overall health of a man does not sharply decline but the types of problems that he has will change. He is not likely to be totally disabled. Metropolitan Life found that "chronic conditions render fewer than 3 percent of all men and women in that age group wholly incapable of carrying out their major activities."[4] People in mid-life are less likely to have allergies, and statistically, have fewer accidents. On the other hand, there is an increase in diabetes between fifty and sixty. Arthritis usually begins after forty. There is an increased likelihood among men for heart attacks and prostate gland problems.

A man's appearance may be the most noticeable physical indicator of his age. His hairline recedes and his hair begins to turn gray. His skin loses its elasticity. Wrinkles become more obvious. Muscles become flabbier, and he moves with less grace as his joints become stiffer.

Weight is a problem for him. The percentage of fat in his total makeup increases. "One study shows [fat] to change from 9.8% of body weight in young men to 21% in men of forty-nine."[5]

HE IS GOING TO LIVE LONGER

The life expectancy of men has increased through the ages. For example, men were said to live only an average of eighteen years in the Bronze Age and only twenty years in ancient Greece. Expectancy had grown to thirty-one in the Middle Ages, thirty-seven by the eighteenth century, and by 1900 in the United States the average was fifty years. Today life expectancy is in the seventies.

If it is true, then, that a man will age more physically than mentally, he needs to shift his energies at mid-life toward developing his mental capacities rather than relying on physical strength.

"Old age can prove to be a great adventure of the spirit, but it can be a torment of the soul if a man steadfastly refuses to think about it until it is upon him. For the name of the Aging Game, obviously, is 'loss.' And whether we win or lose depends upon how well we can handle loss when the time comes: loss of job and status at retirement; loss of mastery over events; loss of control over our children's destiny; loss of vitality—'the death of friends, or death of every brilliant eye that made a catch in the breath,' as Yeats so beautifully expressed it. Now we find out what we're made of."[6]

A man's aging problem has not caught God by surprise, however. God is not primarily youth-oriented; he loves people at every age in life and is concerned to minister to them so their lives continue to be productive as well as contented. Psalm 23 begins, "Because the Lord is my Shepherd, I have everything I need!" The psalm concludes with a deep confidence in God's goodness for all of life and his continued plan for us to be with him after death. "Your goodness and unfailing kindness shall be with me all of my life, and afterwards I will live with you forever in your home."

As a man accepts his own aging process as normal, sees his wife, friends, and God as allies, and shifts his energies toward his mental capacities, he will have reduced some of the nagging pressures of the mid-life crisis.

> But the godly shall flourish like palm trees, and grow tall as the cedars of Lebanon. For they are transplanted into the Lord's own garden, and are under his personal care. Even in old age they will still produce fruit and be vital and green. (Ps. 92:12-14)

22
CHILDREN IN TRANSITION

OUR OLDEST DAUGHTER IS IN her last semester of college, but it feels as though she has been there only about six months. Because my college years were so significant, it seems I was in college about a third of my life. But is she ready to graduate so soon?

Many men in middle life ask the question, "Where did all the time go?" It's easy to feel guilty, because we've spent so much time on our careers and so little on our children.

About this time we feel a strange conflict of emotions. Only yesterday we had been eagerly looking forward to greater and higher achievement. Now we're beginning to look back. Our adolescent children are looking forward with great anticipation to the future, which means independence and their own identity and life-style.

Sadly, it isn't that fathers want to spend more time with their children *now,* but they want to move the clock backward and relive some of those years when the children were younger.

UNDERSTANDING GIVES HOPE

If a man is going to resolve the tension with his adolescent and young-adult offspring, he must learn what they face, how they think, and come to love and respect them. The more we know people and the more they know us, the greater the potential for love.

It is easy for a man to become emotionally separated from his children. He keeps thinking of children in terms of what they were when he was a child—before the Atomic Age, before television, before the new sexual morality. Young people today are aware that more than half the world goes to bed hungry every night. They see, right in their living room, actual wars taking place via television. They are exposed to more choices in school. Drugs are available everywhere. They are led to believe that everybody is involved in sex and alcohol and everyone cheats.

If a man is not aware of what is happening in his children's heads, he is likely to have a great deal of trouble in communication. If he can't communicate, he will probably feel he is failing. This will be a crushing blow to him in mid-life. He will add that to the list of his other failures: he's aging, he's not doing well at work, his marriage seems troubled, and now he can't communicate with his own children. "What's the use of having children anyway?" he may ask.

Communication with his children not only helps a

man understand them, but it also gives the children the opportunity to crystallize their thinking in a healthy, accepting environment. There are some danger signs of which parents should be aware, because they indicate that a child needs greater depth relationship with a mature adult, an opportunity to let it all hang out with an understanding friend who has been there. Blanton warns that "lack of enthusiasm, lack of normal interest in things or people, moodiness, a tendency to be withdrawn and solitary—these are bad signs. So is excessive docility. A child who is always good, who never gets into trouble, who never talks back, is not a normal child."[1]

Perhaps the most helpful thing a father can do is to sit down and *listen* to his child. One of the most productive things we have done with our children through the years is to spend a great deal of time with them at bedtime. This is a casual time when, in the natural flow of conversation, the girls talk about everything that is happening. Sometimes this process has required three hours in an evening, but it has been worth it. Even now, with two of the girls in college, there is a casual sharing at bedtime when they are home. We talk about where they are emotionally and spiritually and the problems that trouble them. Bedtime seems to be a good time for sharing confidences.

STRESS WITH YOUNG ADULTS

"There are few relationships that can be more sensitive than that of a fortyish father and his teen-age son. Each harbors conscious and unconscious feelings of love and hate for the other. The son is emerging from childhood into young adulthood, the father is emerging from young adulthood into middle age."[2]

A man has conflicting attitudes toward his adolescent children. He is proud of his son, and at the same time he is jealous of his strength, his youth, the newness of life before him. He is also proud of his daughter, glad for her brains and beauty. At the same time he may be very jealous that his daughter is willing to give her affection to another man who, of course, is not at all worthy of her.

Sometimes children become judges of their parents. These young adults are extremely idealistic. They go on a hunger fast in order to save food for the world, yet order a pizza at midnight. They get worked up about the energy shortage and are willing to make drastic life-style changes to meet the emergency. They see direct routes to solutions of problems and feel impatient that their parents get distracted by details. They expect perfection in relationships and may have low tolerance for working things out. This idealism of youth demands a lot from a man. The young adult wants ultimate answers now, and dad can only offer worn-out solutions that may seem too tired and too middle-aged.

Sometimes children become very unforgiving and caustic in their judgments. This tends to widen the gap. Bergler records the words of a man who was struggling with his young adult son. "I remember a line from *A Woman of No Importance:* 'Children begin by loving their parents; after a time they judge them; rarely, if ever, do they forgive them.' And remembering this line makes me furious with him all over again."[3]

The problems of adolescent children quite often reawaken unresolved problems from a man's own years of youth. He may be frightened, thinking that somehow he has passed on to his children the anxieties he has never resolved in his own life. Talking with his children may help both a man and his adolescent to work through their anxieties.

CHILDREN BECOME PEOPLE

Children are not playthings, like sports cars, tennis rackets, or sailboats; they are persons. They are not our possessions. It is a man's responsibility from the moment of birth to move his children toward maturity and independence, to enable them to function at every age in life with confidence and effectiveness.

From the moment of birth there should be a gradual transfer of authority to the child, so that by the time the child reaches maturity, he also will have been trained to take responsibility and authority for his own life.

For an adolescent to complete the transition into young adulthood, there must come a major change in the father as well as in the child. They each must be able to look at the other as adults, and their relationship should move increasingly toward an adult relationship instead of "superior parent and inferior adolescent."

This means, as Daniel Levinson says, that fathers will have to "give up their anonymity."[4] It's easy for parents to hide behind the role of a parent and never let the children see them as people. It's easy for the parent always to be ministering down to the child and never allow the child to minister back to the parent. It is easy for the child to always see his father in a position of sufficiency and never get to know him as a real person.

The stress of my mid-life crisis has been helpful to me as a dad and to our daughters. It has been a natural opportunity for them to see me as a very imperfect person with great needs. They have graciously ministered to me and have helped to meet some of my needs.

Some of the stress between a man and his adolescent children will be eased as the marriage relationship is secure and positive. A secure home life tends to reduce frustration and uneasiness in a child's life, and it gives them the ability to cope with pressures more effectively. This is another example of the teeter-totter effect—as a man works on one area of his life, other areas will also be affected. A small improvement helps the other mid-life problems.

A father said to me, with tears in his eyes, "My children don't need me anymore." His children were married, and they *did* need him. No, they didn't need his food and shelter, but they needed him to point the way, to give counsel and wisdom, to help them navigate the emotional and spiritual stresses they would experience throughout their lives. A father should continue to understand his children emotionally and spiritually. He should shift roles from being the director of their lives to being the counseling friend alongside of them. As he does, he will find a continuing place of strategic importance in his children's lives as they move from the adolescent years into young adulthood.

The instruction to fathers in Ephesians is important to note, because the emphasis is not on meeting a child's physical and material needs so much as on being a wise counselor and guide, pointing the way to the child. "And now a word to you [fathers]. Don't keep on scolding and nagging your children, making them angry and resentful. Rather, bring them up with the loving discipline the Lord himself approves, with suggestions and godly advice" (6:4).

BECOMING AN IN-LAW

As young adults move toward marriage, the mid-life man must adjust to a new role, a role of support that does not include interference. The newlyweds need to establish their own family unit. They need to develop their own life-style as a family. The combination of their two backgrounds must now form a new living unit. It is difficult for parents not to give helpful advice when they so desperately want this new marriage to work out perfectly.

Money is usually a problem for a new family. How can parents help financially without tying strings? One family put "a thousand dollars of their savings into a revolving fund for their married children. Any one of the three young families may borrow what it needs without interest, to be paid back as soon as possible, so that the sum may be drawn on by the others when they need it."[5]

No daughter-in-law or son-in-law will ever be quite good enough. This is a common prejudice of parents, but it's important to realize that the son or daughter *chose* this person. One thing that a son or daughter wants very much as they enter into a marriage is to have their parents' approval and, in addition, to have genuine love from them toward the new husband or wife. If the parents see a son-in-law or daughter-in-law as a rival and try to hold the affection of their children, they will not only antagonize the new mate but probably lose the love of their own child as well.

None of our three daughters are married yet, so we don't have firsthand experience with sons-in-law. Our approach, however, over many years has been to develop close, intimate relationships with the girls, to talk freely with them about the important values in marriage and about important qualities to find in a potential mate. Ever since they were born, we have been asking God to mold their lives and the lives of their potential mates so they might have the joy of experiencing a totally satisfying marriage relationship with the man of God's choice for them.

Perhaps the most significant things a man can do to lessen any potential stress with children is to accept them, to come to understand them, to become a friend whom they can trust, to be a person who is not going to put them down, to be interested only in building them up; in short, a person who can love them in the same way Jesus Christ loves us, as he understands our needs and willingly gave himself for us.

O God, you have helped me from my earliest childhood—and I have constantly testified to others of the wonderful things you do. And now that I am old and gray, don't forsake me. Give me time to tell this new generation (and their children too) about all your mighty miracles. (Ps. 71:17-18)

23
PARENTING THE PARENTS

IN MID-LIFE A MAN is likely to have a great deal of anxiety about his responsibility to his aging parents. They have always been the strong generation ahead of him, but now he finds his role changing. They may be in need of his care. (As they need more of his care, it also occurs to him that shortly he will become the oldest generation and in need of care himself.)

Our American society has treated old people with various indignities, "on the one hand, isolating the aged, and letting them know we don't want them and need them, and then at the same time, in the name of medical progress, prolonging their lives beyond the point at which life continues to have meaning to them."[1]

"On certain South Sea islands, feeble male 'senior citizens' were forced to inch their way to the tops of tall coconut palms. The trees were then shaken vigorously by the tribe's young bucks on the ground below. The old boys who managed to hang on were allowed to stay in this world a while longer."[2]

In 1850 only 2.5 percent of the population were over sixty-five years of age. In 1900 the figure was 4 percent; and in 1974, 10.3 percent of the population were over sixty-five.

Older people have become the prey of unscrupulous people selling everything from insurance policies, mutual funds, burial plots, and vitamin pills to sex stimulators, fradulent travel excursions, and faulty hearing aids. The list is almost endless. Sometimes older people are cheated because they are isolated from the rest of society, cut off from information and from other people who could give them wise counsel.

Perhaps one of the biggest indignities an older man faces is when he loses the love relationship with his car. The car, ever since the teen years, has meant masculinity, power, prestige, and authority. Now in his old age the car becomes his master and intimidates him. The highways become frightening. The older man not only gives up driving, but there is a loss of self-worth as he lets his driver's license expire, never to be renewed.

The question that needs to be faced seriously by a man in mid-life is what it means to honor his parents. Does that mean he obeys them in everything, because the Bible tells him God has placed them in authority over him?

The Bible says, "Honor your father and mother (remember, this is a commandment of the Lord your God); if you do so, you shall have a long, prosperous life in the land he is giving you" (Deut. 5:16).

But the Scripture also clearly teaches that there is a transition from childhood to manhood. When a man establishes his own home, he is to leave his father and mother to unite himself in a new emotional unit with his wife.

The concept of honor, however, continues as a responsibility all of a man's life. It is possible for an adult not to do what his parents want him to do and still honor them, appreciate them, and be grateful for who they are and what they have contributed to his life. Obedience is an act that children carry out to their parents for a limited number of years, whereas honor is an attitude that continues all through life.

UNEASY WITH HIS PARENTS?

Repeatedly, I hear couples in their mid-years talking about how their parents still treat them as children. I think of myself as being fairly mature—to a younger generation of students I am somewhat of an authority; to my contemporaries I am thought of as a successful pastor; to some people with emotional problems, I am viewed as a helping person with insight—however, to my parents, I'm still "Jimmy." And for most people in mid-life, that really hurts. They most want to be respected by their parents, but, unfortunately, many times these people who are so important to the man in mid-life still think of him as little Jimmy.

The relationship between older parents and mid-life children is also complicated because, through the childhood and adolescent years, the parents were "the custodians of law and order."[3] The person in mid-life still carries some mixed feeling toward his parents, a sense of fear that is a carry-over from earlier life.

Social class climbing may also cause a breach between

the mid-life "child" and the older parent. Most parents want something better for their children, but they don't realize what will happen in the process. It is not uncommon for a father who did not go to college to urge his son to go on to college and, perhaps, graduate school. The son may then take a job as a professor in a college or a researcher in industry, or he may be a medical doctor. A social separation between this son and his parents naturally comes about. Not only has the son spent more years in school, but he has likely moved upward in social class definitions. Cavan perceptibly points out this problem: "In the upward climb, it is not sufficient that the climber should affiliate himself with the class level above him, assimilating their culture; he must also break his identification with the class level left behind him, most often represented by his parents."[4]

The mid-life "child," who, because of education and job position has moved to a different social class, may have very little in common with his older parents, who were really the promoters of a better way of life for him. Tragically, when they get together, they talk about areas that essentially mean nothing to either of them, because these are the only areas on which they have common ground.

WHERE WILL OUR PARENTS LIVE?

Perhaps the biggest problem that people in mid-life and their older parents face is where the parents will live. Should they move to Maranatha Village, continue to live in their own home, or move in with their married children? This question can cause everyone in the family to get upset at everyone else. Brothers, sisters, and parents

257

may well be angry and disappointed with one another

One reason this problem is difficult to answer is that there are so many possible solutions. Sometimes living in the child's home is the happiest solution for everyone. Some older parents feel more secure in their own home with familiar surroundings. Other times the retirement village is the ideal solution, and then again it is necessary to think of a special-care facility. It must be a common decision of every person involved.

Tragically, the most frequent pattern is one of "Let's not talk about it." If we talk about it, parents may feel hurt or that they are being cast away. The mid-life children may feel guilty if the arrangement the parents want does not seem feasible to the children, so everyone simply keeps smiling and pretending that no one is getting older.

Closely related to this is financial support. Again, everyone should be involved in these decisions and the discussion about Medicaid, Social Security, investments, and savings. Then the older parents don't have to be frightened about lack of money or inability to care for themselves.

PARENTS CONTINUE TO MINISTER

People are marrying at an earlier age, families are smaller, childbearing is completed earlier, and at the same time, life is being extended. "Tomorrow's families will normally include both sets of grandparents, and a great-grandparent or two, making four generations."[5]

One problem I see in young people is that they are rootless, living only "now," with no sense of history or continuity toward future generations. Grandparents can minister significantly to help with this problem. They can give the children "unity of family life and some knowledge of their own family history. . . . The memory of a grandparent may span 150 years of family history."[6]

A grandparent can also be strategic spiritually in the extended family. One of the people who most influenced me during my adolescent and young-adult years was my grandmother, Mary. In old age she did not quietly retire to the back room, feeling sorry for herself. She was an extremely exuberant woman whom I really never saw as old.

Grandma used all kinds of circumstances to minister to me personally. One time as a young boy I was responsible for raking all the leaves in our backyard. I'm sure the task wasn't very great, but from my perspective it was as if I'd been asked to clean up the whole city of Cleveland. My grandmother, who lived across the fence from us, saw me leaning on the rake. She came over, put her arm around me, and said, "I'll help you. We'll get it done."

She was also the one who continually asked me where I was spiritually. She was the one who most influenced my decision to receive Christ as Savior and my decision to enter the ministry. Grandma and grandpa ministered intensively to me, as they did to all the other grandchildren. At the same time, they continued to minister to their own children and to the new sons- and daughters-in-law.

THE DEATH OF PARENTS

Dr. Abraham Maslow said, "One learns more from the death of a parent than from all the academic subjects one studies."[7] When a man's parents are still living, he is more protected from his own death, because he always thinks they will die first. When his parents are gone, he unconsciously knows he is next in line; in fact, he's the first of the line.

LeShan, speaking of the death of a parent, says,

> This can be a time of profound growth and change, if one allows oneself truly to experience all the rich variety of mournful, ambivalent, guilty feelings, as well as the new awareness of how deeply one has been influenced by one's parents, and how much they are part of oneself—often more in death than even in life. The death of a parent opens up new avenues of insight and perception about dependency, mortality—and immortality—the meaning of love and acceptance, the importance of remembering human frailty as well as strength—the meaning of 'family'—how that includes memories and relationships that suddenly take on new and deeper significance. The inner work of accepting and using such a separation for one's own maturation may add greatly to one's stature in middle age. Discovering that it is terrible to be a motherless child even at the age of fifty teaches you some important lessons about the human condition.[8]

ATTITUDES ARE IMPORTANT

The book *In-Laws—Pros and Cons* by Evelyn Duvall offers a number of good insights into the in-law relationship and lists some of the attitudes necessary to produce positive relationships between parents and their married children. It's important, she says, that mid-life children see their parents as persons with needs. As the mid-life child understands his parents' needs and seeks to make these parents feel significant, a relationship of love will develop. If the parents are treated as castaways and unimportant, however, antagonism and animosity will grow.

There is the story of the mid-life father who sent his older adolescent son to the attic to get the old horse blanket. He explained to his son that grandpa was getting very old and cantankerous, so they were going to send him away. The heavy horse blanket was to be used to keep him warm as he rode away in the buggy.

A few minutes later the son returned with half of the blanket and handed it to his father. The mid-life father in startled amazement asked, "What happened to the blanket?"

The adolescent son replied, "I'm saving the other half for you."

Old people—anyone for that matter—need to feel that their lives have meaning, that they are contributing to life, and that they are loved. A man's attitudes toward his parents can have a great part in meeting those needs.

> But our families will continue; generation after generation will be preserved by your protection. (Ps. 102:28)

24
CREATIVE RETIREMENT

SOMETIME IN MID-LIFE A MAN grasps the brutal truth—society is moving him toward retirement. He may be pressured, enticed, or shoved into an early retirement by his company, which pleasantly suggests that he might like to live out his years from fifty-five on doing all the things he always wanted to do. The truth is, some businesses have a planned program of obsolescence. Early retirement is a deeply ingrained concept to make room for younger people coming up from the bottom.

The prospect of retirement, even though highly praised, means a loss in self-esteem to most men. Earlier we pointed out that a man's work is often equated with worth. So he must now face the truth that society is going to do all it can to push him into retirement.

Our society seems to be one of the first to force the retirement idea onto people. There is certainly no concept of retirement, as we know it, in the Bible. The Bible does show that men change as they move along through life, and their responsibilities and activities change; but there is no biblical concept of sitting on the back porch rocking away several good years of your life.

The Bible does speak of retirement that comes after death: "At last the time has come for his martyrs to enter into their full reward. Yes, says the Spirit, they are blest indeed, for now they shall rest from all their toils and trials" (Rev. 14:13).

The Bible does teach that people need periodic rest, sometimes for extended periods of time. Jesus said every person needs emotional and spiritual rest. He gave us an invitation: "Come to me and I will give you rest—all of you who work so hard beneath a heavy yoke. Wear my yoke—for it fits perfectly—and let me teach you; for I am gentle and humble, and you shall find rest for your souls; for I give you only light burdens" (Matt. 11:28-30). So the Bible does teach that there is a final rest after death as well as various periods of physical, emotional, and spiritual rest all along through life. But no rocking chair is envisioned.

If a man interacts with the mid-life crisis fully, it can be the most profitable experience to prepare him for his own retirement. As he comes to a peaceful self-image, an enthusiastic relationship with his mate, as he adjusts his career to fit his life and works through pressures with his children and parents, he will find that this emotional work is the best preparation for what society calls retirement. If, on the other hand, a man does not face these concerns in mid-life, they will grow, and when he is pushed out of a job, it will be as if the world collapses around him.

QUESTIONS FOR NONRETIREMENT

Mid-life is the time to begin asking the questions about life-style and activities in our later years. If possible, a man should never retire. In order not to, however, he has to plan now so he can make the necessary transition from his present work into "nonretirement." If a man believes God is going to continually use him and his abilities, he can prepare now.

1. *Where should he live?* A man has been helping his parents decide where they should live, and this research and evaluation should provide the basis for his own decision. Where to live should not only include the area of the country or of the world but also the kind of housing.

A creative solution to this problem may be to get three or four other friends to jointly purchase a small apartment building. This may lower the cost of living for each couple.

The retirement village my father started in Sebring, Florida, is a good example of nonretirement. We jokingly tease my dad that people work harder when they move there than if they had stayed in their own houses. It is sort of an unwritten expectation that everyone in the village is going to work—building more apartments, planting trees or grass, painting walls, making roads and driveways, and helping people move in. In a continuously expanding project such as Maranatha Village, there is always work to be done, and as a result, people continue to feel important and useful.

2. *Style of living* is another question that will influence the size and location of living quarters. It will also influence automobile ownership, recreational activities, and travel. If a couple envisions traveling regularly to other countries, owning a new automobile each year, and liv-

ing in a large estate, they need to prepare now for that expensive style. If the couple, however, plans more modest experiences, they also need to learn to live modestly before they get to the time when they must.

3. *Money* will be a major concern, and careful planning at mid-life will be critical. After a man has decided where he wants to live and what style he wants to follow, then he needs to evaluate his savings, investments, pension plans, and Social Security benefits. He should consider how much money all of these plans will produce and, with continued inflation, what he actually will have to live on when the time comes.

Without being too pessimistic, it's important to remember that he must carefully investigate the dollar resources in which he is placing his trust. For example, most pensions are not transferable from one company to another. If a man decides to move to another career, he may lose many years of pension.

Savings are another example of a financial source with false security. A man may feel greatly elated that he is earning 6 or 7 percent on long-term savings. What he fails to take into account is that he is paying income tax on the earnings plus losing a certain portion to inflation, so his savings are continually shrinking in buying power.

Money sources must somehow be tied to inflation so that when a man needs them, they will buy as much then as they would buy now.

4. *Working* should not be an option, but it ought to be part of the long-range plan. Working may not be for the purpose of earning money, but a man must continue to contribute to society.

Older people were asked, "If you inherited enough money to live comfortably for the rest of your life, would you continue to work?" The response was a unanimous "Yes."[1]

5. Following the evaluation of these areas, a man and wife should lay out *a program of small steps* that will lead to their ultimate goals. Part of this plan may mean using vacations to explore various parts of the country in which they would consider living. They may begin talking with other friends about the possibility of pooling resources for later years. They may shift their investments or seek new investments. More education or job training may be needed to gain new skills for the years of nonretirement. Long-range planning will also include the children and their families so that regular contact and communication can be maintained.

At this point a man must also consider the unexpected death of himself or his wife. What would his wife do if he dies first (which is likely to happen, according to statistics)? How would this affect the nonretirement years, and what specific steps and directions should his wife follow? This process may be called "Teaching My Wife to Be a Widow During Retirement."

The retirement plan may be altered over the years, but without a plan, a man simply drifts along toward retirement and, perhaps, toward frustrating chaos.

> Jehovah himself is caring for you! He is your defender. He protects you day and night. He keeps you from all evil, and preserves your life. He keeps his eye upon you as you come and go, and always guards you. (Ps. 121:5-8)

25
SOONER OR LATER

INTELLECTUALLY, WE ALL KNOW that people die, but before mid-life we tend to think of death in terms of *other* people. Suddenly, in mid-life some event or thought causes us to realize that death is going to happen to us.

I was at Fuller Seminary working on my doctorate when my wife called me late one night and told me that Gaston Singh had died of a massive heart attack. The news hit me like a sledgehammer. Gaston was only in his mid-thirties. Two weeks earlier he and his family had stayed in our home. In 1975 Sally and I had spent a month ministering in India, Bangladesh, and Burma with Gaston and another close friend. In a few months I was to return to India to minister with him again, but now he was gone! Everything had changed.

In retrospect, that death and my turning forty-five only days before seemed to be the two incidents that plunged me deep into my mid-life crisis.

I had helped many other people through the stress related to death. I knew what the Bible taught: "No man can live forever. All will die. Who can rescue his life from the power of the grave?" (Ps. 89:48). The Bible not only teaches that everyone is going to die or be taken directly when Christ returns, but also that our time of death is uncertain. "How do you know what is going to happen tomorrow? For the length of your lives is as uncertain as the morning fog—now you see it; soon it is gone" (James 4:14).

Suddenly death became real for me. Freud said, "No one believes in his own death. In the unconscious, everyone is convinced of his immortality."[1] But now I began thinking not in terms of how many years I had lived but how many I might have left.

HOW DOES A MAN SEE HIS OWN DEATH?

In mid-life, as death takes on more real meaning, there seem to be four major ways in which men cope with the reality of their own death.

1. A man may deny that he is going to die because death is linked with old age and, if he is still trying to deny the aging process, he will find it difficult to accept the reality of death for him. Paul Tournier, the Swiss Christian psychiatrist, links acceptance of old age and death: "I could not dissociate acceptance of old age from that of death. The two problems are so intimately bound up together that we may say that acceptance of old age is the best preparation for death, but also, conversely, that the acceptance of death is the best preparation for old age."[2]

2. A man may accept defeat. Our culture treats death as abnormal. We rush people off to the hospital, sedate them heavily, and isolate them from everyone so no one will have to be exposed to death. A man may be so discouraged by the reality of his ultimate death that he may give up the desire to continue living. A Greek poet in the seventh century B.C. wrote:

> When the springtime of life is past
> then verily to die is better than life.
> For many are the ills that invade the heart.[3]

3. Men may find themselves oppressively overcome with the fear of death. "The idea of death, the fear of it, haunts the human animal like nothing else," says the Pulitzer Prize winner Ernest Becker.[4] This fear may come because they are unprepared to face life after death and to have their lives evaluated by a righteous God. Fear may come because of a lack of information about what happens in death. "Does it hurt to die? Will I still want to live even when I'm dying?"

Every man must work through each of these anxieties, getting factual information to prepare for the stage of acceptance. A man needs to settle his standing with God so he has peace about meeting him.

4. Acceptance of death takes many forms. Some grant a grudging acceptance, such as W. C. Fields, who had these words chiseled on his tombstone: "I'd rather be in Philadelphia."[5] He was saying, in essence, that he looked at death, didn't like it, and would rather ignore it; but he would have to accept it.

Coming fully to accept one's ultimate death gives a serene quality to life and prepares a person to enjoy life more completely. Abraham Maslow shared his feelings after he had a heart attack:

The confrontation with death—and the reprieve from it—makes everything look so precious, so sacred, so beautiful that I feel more strongly than ever the impulse to love it, to embrace it, and to let myself be overwhelmed by it. My river has never looked so beautiful. . . . Death, and its ever present possibility makes love, passionate love, more possible. I wonder if we could love passionately, if ecstasy would be possible at all, if we knew we'd never die.[6]

During mid-life a man must not only peacefully accept the reality of his own death, but he also has to accept the fact that his mate may die before he does. If he can accept this, then he'll find a measure of freedom and joy in the marriage relationship. There is a valuing of hours and days that gives a special, loving intensity that might not be realized if the death of one's mate is feared or denied.

An interesting phenomenon takes place through the mid-life crisis. At the beginning, a man apparently is very preoccupied with the possibility of his death. During the crisis, he hopefully moves to a peaceful acceptance of his own mortality. As he enters that third major productive era of life, the preoccupation with death loses its grip of him. His new emphasis is to live life to the fullest and minister to people.

The Scriptures can be extremely important in helping a man face this major concern in mid-life. The Bible teaches that when we place our personal trust in Christ, God the Holy Spirit comes to live in us during this life. Death is only a transition to a continued experience of living with God. In John 14 and 17, Jesus expressed very clearly that God is planning for each believer to be with him for eternity.

I Corinthians 15 teaches us about the resurrection of men and life after death eternally with God. The chapter concludes with these ringing words, "So, my dear brothers, since future victory is sure, be strong and steady, always abounding in the Lord's work, for you know that nothing you do for the Lord is ever wasted as it would be if there were no resurrection" (v. 58).

Building a model airplane is much the same as a man working his way through the concerns of the mid-life crisis. If he says he will work on all of the other concerns except his marriage or some other particular area, it is like saying he will build his airplane but won't build any wings. Each part of the plane takes time to build, and each part is difficult in its own way; yet each part contributes to making the airplane able to fly.

I remember from my boyhood days working long, tedious hours in gluing every stick of a model airplane in place and carefully covering the frame with paper. My plane had been correctly constructed so that it would fly perfectly. There was a special exhilaration in going to the third-floor attic window and watching my newly made masterpiece soar into the sky. My heart went with it.

"Fly, man, fly!"

> Death stared me in the face—I was frightened and sad. Then I cried, "Lord, save me!" How kind he is! How good he is! So merciful, this God of ours! (Ps. 116:3-5)

PART 7

HELP IS ON THE WAY

26
WE CAN HELP

THE MAN IN MID-LIFE IS up to his armpits in quicksand. The more he struggles, the deeper he sinks. He is struggling with a real crisis. He may well have tried several dead-end roads. He is hopefully working to improve several major areas of his life, but help must also come from the outside, and he must be willing to accept that help.

He may respond almost indifferently to outside help. He may use indifference to reinforce people's thinking about how bad-off he really is. However, his indifference ought to be overlooked and help offered anyway.

Help can come from several different sources and, hopefully, from all of them, including his employer, the church, his children, friends, and his wife.

A MAN'S EMPLOYER

An employer can best help a man by realizing that the crisis through which he is going is just that—a short-term crisis. When he is through the crisis, he will continue to be a productive employee and probably will be more valuable because he has an increased perspective and deeper desire to serve.

It may also be very strategic for an employer to offer an employee the possibility of a job change within the organization to better meet his career aspirations.

An employer can be helpful by suggesting further education or training so that the man's skills can improve. A new challenge will strengthen his self-image, which has been under severe attack during the crisis.

The employer may encourage him to seek counseling help from someone on the company payroll or from community services through the company medical provisions.

The biggest help I received from my employer—that is, the church—was their understanding. The Board of Leadership said, in essence, "We don't really know from experience what you are going through [most of them are much younger than I], but we love you and we want you to tell us how we can help." That open attitude provided a great deal of strength for me and reduced the pressure of performance on the job.

THE CHURCH

The mid-life crisis is almost publicly unknown in the church, although many members are going through the problems.

The church needs to recognize that this crisis is a significant developmental problem that all adults face. We have youth workers to work full time with adolescents because we recognize that to be a key time of life. We hire full-time music directors and Christian education directors, and some churches have full-time business administrators. But this major crisis continues to fester secretly in each mid-life individual's heart, each one thinking he is the only strange person experiencing this kind of stress and trying to work through it alone. There is no special staff person to help him.

The church needs to become more vocal on this issue. More family conferences need to be set up, with the mid-life problem included. Couples' retreats and Sunday school classes need to discuss the crisis. Retreats for men only and women only need to have this topic as the major discussion.

Over the years I have watched scores of people in mid-life quietly slip out the back door of the church. Each one felt he was a failure—morally or spiritually—and most of all, emotionally. He had been taught all of his life that being a Christian would guarantee that no problem would ever defeat him. When the mid-life crisis hit, he was literally flattened as if in a boxing match. As he lifted his head from the canvas and staggered to his feet, he looked at the church filled with people who seemed to be so successful and cocksure of themselves. He saw people with whom he was afraid to speak, people who would have only compounded his guilt. He saw a church speaking about forgiveness, love, and acceptance, but he didn't experience any of that. So, disillusioned, he quietly walked away to his dressing room and out into the night in a different direction.

One of the difficult things I have had to carry as a pastor is the secret burdens of people who are hurting in the church. In a large church, there is always one—and many times several—wrestling with unmentionable areas of the mid-life crisis. Sometimes it is almost emotionally overwhelming for me to know what people are experiencing and not be able to share that with anyone.

As the church grows in an attitude of acceptance, as they talk more freely about the mid-life crisis, and as they offer genuine forgiveness to people who have failed, some of these people will turn back to the church and find it to be a community of strength and support.

A pastor friend called me recently and shared a difficult problem. Two of the officials in his church, a married man and a divorced woman, are secretly having an affair. What does he do? Does he tell the board? Does he put the couple out of the church? What if it all blows open and he has kept it a secret?

The church needs to move away from blame fixing and jump in to meet needs. The person in the mid-life crisis needs a friend, not an accuser. I Corinthians says that the church is to function like a body: "If one part suffers, all parts suffer with it, and if one part is honored, all the parts are glad" (I Cor. 12:26). A man needs friends who are willing to accept him and suffer with him.

During the time I have been going through the mid-life crisis myself, I have freely shared my anxieties with the church. Sometimes I felt that all I was talking about were my depressing struggles, or I was illustrating my sermons only from my own conflicts. Yet, the more I shared, the more other mid-life men and women began to verbalize their own frustrations.

I feel there was a lack in my seminary training; I was not taught how to cope with people in mid-life. When I was a young pastor, I could not adequately minister to people at this time in life because I did not understand their problem.

As the church, including its pastors and leaders, becomes vocal and helps people through the mid-life crisis, we will see a great deal of strength being preserved in the church. Mid-life people won't want to be slipping out the back door.

A MAN'S CHILDREN

For children in the family to help a father, they need first to have some idea of what he is going through. More than understanding what is happening, however, they need to commit themselves to helping. This commitment will not only move the man through his crisis, but it will also help the adolescent children to mature as they minister to their father.

It is important for the children not to withdraw and treat dad as though he has typhoid fever. They can strengthen him by allowing him to continue his role as leader and counselor in the home. They can remind him of how much they appreciate him and mention specific things that will build his self-esteem. Even though he may seem to reject their words when he is in the depth of his despondency, the building remarks do carry an overall positive effect. The children can agree together to pray that God will successfully move their dad through this crisis. Jesus said, "I also tell you this—if two of you agree down here on earth concerning anything you ask for, my Father in heaven will do it for you" (Matt. 18:19). (My wife and daughters often had to claim verses such as this when there was little else to lean on.)

My children have each been extremely sensitive to me during this time of my need. They have repeatedly sought opportunities to minister to me. Typical of these expressions of love was a story written by one of my daughters and given to me as a Christmas gift. It expresses the girls' appreciation of me as well as their love and support:

> Once there lived a man in a quaint harbor town who repaired ships. He was known by nearly everyone, because he was the most skilled craftsman for miles around. Often he would repair damaged boats for no charge at all. He worked on sailboats of all sizes and types. When a sailboat would become unseaworthy, it would be brought straight to him. Ships were brought that had been torn by bad weather, had collided with other ships, had been misused, or even boats that were never built properly in the first place. He would take each one and soon have it ready to sail again.
>
> The man was a great artisan and had been in constant apprenticeship all of his life to the Master Craftsman. The Master Craftsman was a builder of ships; in fact, he was the most skilled builder ever to have lived. The Master Craftsman taught the man the art of repairing broken ships and, because they were such close friends, the Master Craftsman even taught him how to build his own ships.
>
> The man always seemed to have dozens of damaged ships he was working on at once, and more always waiting. Often the man would work years to rebuild a single ship, working day and night.
>
> Many times he would become discouraged, for he saw only broken ships. He longed to leap aboard a fine new ship and sail toward the Morning Star. He longed to feel the free breeze at his face and the salt-foam about his feet.
>
> The man's fame continued to grow and often he was called to other port cities to work. Everything he did flourished. Many other men became apprentices to him and his work increased. Through his work and teaching, more and more ships were repaired each year.
>
> Now, although this man worked most of his life at re-

building ships, his greatest work was not the remaking of broken sailboats, but it was the building of three beautiful new ships. These were his greatest pride and showed all of his finest artisan craftsmanship, because into these three ships the man had put his life and love.

A MAN AND HIS FRIENDS

Friends are likely to come in for a lot of abuse during a man's mid-life crisis, but they are extremely important in helping him through this time. If a friend will hang on and continue to minister, the friendship is likely to move into a new depth after the crisis is over.

The man in mid-life crisis will probably have little time for friends. If he is in the stage of trying to relive his young-adult years, he will not have much in common with the friends near his age. As he moves into the depression and withdrawal stages, he will not want to be bothered with his friends and will give all kinds of excuses, such as, it is just too much work getting together; he is bored with life; he doesn't really enjoy doing that anymore; those people were never really his friends anyway.

The quality of friendship will quickly be seen during this time. Friends with whom he has a surface relationship will drop away. Other friends who are using him, or whom he is using, to gain some political or social status will probably back off during this period.

True, caring friends are likely to surface at this time. Friendships such as David and Jonathan's in the Old Testament tend to grow under pressure, because there is a desire in each one to meet the other one's need rather than to use the other. David said, when he heard of the death of his friend Jonathan,

These mighty heroes have fallen in the midst of battle.
Jonathan is slain upon the hills.
How I weep for you, my brother Jonathan;
How much I loved you!
And your love for me was deeper
Than the love of woman! (2 Sam. 1:25-26)

During my crisis, a number of people cared for me. It was difficult for me to change roles and let others minister to me instead of my ministering to them. There were times when I felt it was a sign of weakness to let them care for me, but in truth it deepened our friendship.

After my month's leave of absence from the church, I told the Board of Leadership that what I most appreciated in their friendship was that they hung onto me with confidence and hope in prayer and friendship when I didn't seem to be able to hang on for myself. Proverbs 17:17 says, "A true friend is always loyal, and a brother is born to help in time of need."

A man is likely to have new attitudes toward people as he experiences deep and genuine support from friends. He will be a more sympathetic man and be willing to extend himself in caring for others because of the care he has experienced.

A man's friends in life from this point on are not likely to be the type of people he will exploit or the type who will use him. They probably will be people who genuinely minister to him and to whom he can minister.

Several people I know right now are going through various stages of the mid-life crisis. One is involved in an affair, another is in divorce court, another's wife has left him, and others are in similar stress. Each of these people, perhaps facing the greatest pressures they have known in their life, *do not have one friend* to stand with them.

It is not important for a man to have many friends during the crisis, but one friend can be truly significant and turn the tide from hopelessness and despair toward direction and meaning.

A WIFE CAN HELP

The one human being who can be the most help to a man during his mid-life crisis is his wife. He may get help from work, counselors, Christians in the church, his children, or friends, but his wife is still going to be the most strategic person to help him.

Unfortunately, helping her husband will probably be the most difficult task she has ever had in her life. If at the time she is wrestling with her own problems, the requirements for helping her husband may put such a great strain on the marriage that it could fall apart.

What a wife needs at first is a knowledge of the problem. She "should view [the crisis] as a stage in the developmental process, not as a kind of flu. You are not talking about something so simple as mere dissatisfaction. You are talking about an existential condition."[1]

She may feel that "a nightmare has somehow intruded into their previously peaceful and pleasant lives."[2] If she doesn't understand the overall crisis, she is likely to believe everything her husband says about her and that his crisis is her fault.

A woman needs to be prepared for the widely vascillating moods her husband will be going through. "It's like riding a roller-coaster of interpersonal relations, with dips and swirls, switchbacks and terrifying dives."[3]

A wife should be prepared to be blamed for her husband's depression and for his bad marriage. He may say,

"I want happiness, love, approval, admiration, sex, youth. All this is denied me in this stale marriage to an elderly, sickly, complaining, nagging wife."[4]

A man is likely to strongly affirm that "*he* is not aging and failing to make the necessary allowances; it is *she* who is responsible for all that and wants to drag him down."[5]

In a letter to the editors of *Medical Economics*, a physician's wife wrote that her husband was experiencing all of the symptoms of the male mid-life crisis. The editors recommended psychiatric treatment. There followed a flood of letters from men who strongly disagreed with the advice given to the woman: "Almost to a man, the writers agreed that the primary cause. . . . was neither his hormones nor his neuroses nor his environment but, in fact, his wife!"[6] A wife is going to need a great deal of strength to handle this unrighteous onslaught from her husband as he lists her failures.

Sometimes the wife during the crisis will fill the leadership vacuum and will begin to dominate the home and her husband. This is a time in a woman's life when her own self-assertion will be very strong. If she does become dominant and domineering, she is likely to impede her husband's progress as he works his way through his mid-life crisis.

It's easy for a wife to slip into a mothering role when she sees her husband hurting. Part of his nature cries out for that kind of care, but the wife must be careful that she not be viewed by her husband as his mother. It is possible for her to give loving support as a friend, as a lover, and as a wife without becoming his mother. If he identifies her as his mother, he is apt to reject her, because during the mid-life crisis he is looking more for the girlfriend type than the mother type.

Being attractive. The ultimate quality a man wants in a

wife for the long-term relationship is a woman who is concerned for his needs, according to a survey reported in *Reader's Digest*.[7] But during his mid-life crisis, he may very well be looking for other qualities. Some of the common complaints of men at this age are that their wives aren't attractive, don't turn them on sexually, are old, and don't understand. It's important for a woman during her husband's crisis to work on her own physical attractiveness, including weight and muscle tone; improve her wardrobe; and alter her life-style a bit to more nearly fit the changing needs her husband is feeling.

Perhaps at no other time in their married life is she so likely to be in competition with other women. So, even though the quality of caring is going to be the characteristic a man wants long-range, she must be attractive to him during the short-range crisis period.

If a wife can swing with the punches and hang onto her sanity, she'll make it through the mid-life crisis with her husband, and they likely will stay married. One statistical study showed that "despite what their fantasies might be, men were not dashing off to marry young women. Only some 2.9 per cent of men aged forty-five to fifty-four were married to women under the age of thirty-four."[8]

A psychiatrist remarks, "The wife is stronger than she knows. . . . In approximately ninety per cent of these cases one can be pretty sure the situation will not end in divorce."[9]

Learning to help. Dr. Bergler in *The Revolt of the Middle-Aged Man* records part of an interview with a wife who asked how she could help her husband. He said, " 'First, find out what it is all about. Secondly, be patient. Thirdly, don't reproach him.' She interrupted: 'Fourthly, be an angel.' Her voice was heavy with sarcasm. [He continued,] 'It's tough, but rewarding. The chances are you are in no danger of losing your husband.' "[10]

The wife needs to find ways to gently draw her husband out of his cave of silence. He doesn't like to be alone, but he doesn't know how to share the pain he is feeling. "The strange truth is that when a man has to retreat into silence before his wife, he experiences a sense of disappointment. This is in fact the last thing he wants to do."[11]

A woman can help her husband during this time by building his self-image, reminding him of the areas in which he is successful. He may outwardly reject her attempts, and she may feel tempted to tell him to quit feeling sorry for himself, but her encouragement will help to maintain his self-esteem.

Encouraging him to attempt new areas of growth will be another positive way in which a wife can assist. She may help him think about new career alternatives, suggest that he return for more study or training in his special skills, or encourage him to learn new skills he would like to acquire.

There are times when a man wants to be alone and simply stare out the window. Those times, especially during the depression and withdrawal phases of the crisis, are important. The wife should allow him to experience some of those times. She can also help by encouraging him to go for a bike ride, a walk, or a ride in the car or the boat. Or she may be able to gently involve one or two friends for short periods of time to keep him in touch with the outside world.

A man's wife can help him by keeping herself emotionally strong. She needs to have a good talking relationship with a friend and with God, both of whom can give her perspective on what is happening and encouragement when the bottom seems to drop out.

Perhaps the most effective thing the wife can do is "to

be able to join him in his problems. It's not enough for her to find new ways to look nice, or to try to be sexier. She has to recognize the despair he may be feeling."[12]

What a wife most needs is perspective from God. Isaiah 43:1-3 says, "Don't be afraid, for I have ransomed you; I have called you by name; you are mine. When you go through deep waters and great trouble, I will be with you. When you go through rivers of difficulty, you will not drown! When you walk through the fire of oppression, you will not be burned up—the flames will not consume you. For I am the Lord your God, your Savior." Sometimes all that will keep a wife going is confidence in God's love and ability. And that, after all, is the ultimate solution.

> Pity me, O Lord, for I am weak. Heal me, for my body is sick, and I am upset and disturbed. My mind is filled with apprehension and with gloom. Oh, restore me soon.
>
> Come, O Lord, and make me well. In your kindness save me. (Ps. 6:2-4)

27
A MAN HELPS HIMSELF

WHEN I WAS IN MY MID-TEENS, I went on a fishing trip to Canada with my mom, dad, and brother. We were about an hour out of camp as I sat peacefully in the front of the boat, casting out my line. Suddenly my mother wound up with a giant sidearm cast and buried the hooks of her lure in my back. I felt as if I had been hit with a four-inch steel pipe. The shock was unbelievable.

My reaction thirty years later to the mid-life crisis was much the same. I was totally unprepared for what happens to men. Yes, I had seen other men struggle with similar problems; I had been involved in helping many of them, but I had always believed this crisis came upon them because of some inherent failing in their lives. I thought of myself as relatively mature, well educated, growing emotionally, and in a deep relationship with God.

In spite of all these positive assets, the crisis still came. Only after it hit me and I began to read about it did I realize that people working in the area of human development and behavior are convinced that this crisis hits every man to some degree.

As I talk to people in their twenties and thirties and share with them what I have been through, they unanimously believe it won't happen to them, or they hope that somehow they can avoid it. Barbara Fried found this to be true also. "Younger adults, particularly those in their twenties and early thirties, are puzzled by his symptoms and skeptical about their reality. A thirty-two-year-old, for example, dismissed the idea of the crisis by saying flatly, 'But that'll never happen to me, I'm sure of it. I have never been a ladies' man.' It's difficult to convince a twenty-year-old that someone two decades his elder cherishes the same romantic fantasies he himself has only recently outgrown and discarded. . . . 'When I'm that old, I'll know better than to be running around and having affairs.' "[1]

A person in his twenties is so filled with idealism and beginning his career that he simply doesn't have time to think about the developmental problems of mid-life. After all, ten to twenty years for a young adult seems as far away as the moon. The man in his thirties is so busy achieving his idealized goals that he doesn't take time to stop and think, and if he does pause to reflect, he reasons that if he tries harder, he'll avoid the crisis.

In spite of the fact that men in their twenties and thirties will probably not listen to my tale, I believe it is the obligation of educators and the church to begin preparing men and women for the mid-life transitional crisis.

ATTITUDES I WOULD NEED

After the fishhooks had been buried in my back, my father said I had some choices to make. (One choice we didn't discuss was to pretend that I didn't have the hooks in my back. The truth was obvious to everyone: I had a problem.) Dad told me I could either endure the agony of an hour traveling back to shore and then an additional hour driving into town to find a doctor, or I could allow my dad to cut the hooks out right on the spot. He said all I would need was a little bravery.

That's the way I came to feel about the mid-life crisis. I began reading about all of the attitudes I would need in order to make it through the crisis, but the question was how would I get those attitudes? Neugarten said I needed "cathectic flexibility," "ego differentiation," "body transcendence," and "sexual integration," among other things.[2] John McLeish in *The Ulyssean Adult* said I should be "emotionally intensely alive."[3] Joel and Lois Davitz in *Making It from 40 to 50* said my behavior "is not merely selfish or silly. [The] sometimes astonishing variety of behaviors is part of an overall pattern of personal development."[4] Fried told me it was nothing but a "developmental crisis"; it had a beginning, and it would have an ending.[5] Daniel Levinson cautioned me to do more than simply tough it out. He said, "The fact is that there is something very profound happening here. . . . I mean: Take it seriously, man! Don't just say, 'If I can hold out, I'll be all right.' "[6]

The experts continued with Erikson suggesting that I needed to move into "generativity."[7] Kenn Rogers said I should not run from my problem but rather "fight it."[8] Tournier said the struggle was good for me: "Our life, then, has a meaning for us when we have a definite goal, when we struggle to attain it."[9] Sheehy also said I needed the crisis and I should "let it happen."[10]

Eda LeShan said the mid-life crisis is like the Dark Ages; following that would be Renaissance: ". . . a time of re-birth, and birth is full of struggle."[11] Hunt said the mid-life crisis is like the mid-course correction of a rocket in order to help it reach its goal.[12] For a while I wished I had been a Menomini Indian, because Slotkin told me they had no problems in mid-life.[13]

People were giving me all kinds of newspaper and magazine articles. Most of these articles were trying to joke me out of my problem—Judith Viorst's article, "How Do You Know When You're 40?"[14] Josephine Lowman's "Don't Think 'Middle Age,' "[15] and a very funny article by Davis Matheny of the *Minneapolis Star*, "Is There Life After 40?" His approach was to show that anyone younger than forty was really dumb: "Never praise the 'vitality' of underaged people. When somebody else does—and those who do are usually trying to show how young-thinking they are—say nothing, but let a look of inexpressible boredom glaze over your features. Our research shows that people under 25 usually move about like tree-sloths, and the majority of them, like everyone else, are no more original and fresh in their thinking than rutabagas."[16]

The problem with all of these helpful suggestions is that I was becoming more depressed. It seemed that other people were making it, but I was not. My attitude was clearly one of self-pity. Because I didn't know how to help myself, I wanted to give up. Bergler jumped in and said that "resignation" is not the way out,[17] and yet that was the only way that seemed possible for me.

The people that put the most pressure on me were the ones who told me, by subtle remark or direct statement, that if I were a better Christian I wouldn't be having these troubles. These people were like Job's comforters, telling me that if I'd just confess all my sins to God, I wouldn't be going through all these troubles. I felt like strangling them! One such comment came from a minister who distributed this idea on a tape. He said people who have a personal relationship with Jesus Christ "have the least amount of problems. They are not threatened really, at any of these levels, because they recognize the purpose of God in their life and are rounded out at the psyche level with the proper inputs."[18] All of these suggestions have ultimately been helpful, but for most of the crisis period, they simply intimidated me and made me feel like a greater failure.

WHAT SEEMED TO HELP ME

1. Physical exercise seemed to clear out my mind and drain off some of the emotional tension. It was great to get on my daughter's ten-speed bike and head out into the country. It seemed to flush out my personality. I would come back physically tired, but the tiredness seemed good. Walking also was helpful, many times with Sally, but quite often alone. My office is a mile from our home, and on a number of occasions I would jog home. Each of these things seemed to help for brief periods of time.

2. I began to take on some new challenges. One was education. I started working on a doctorate at Fuller Seminary. When I got there for the first course, I found that a large proportion of the men in the program were also obviously wrestling with the mid-life crisis. The explosion of adult education indicates that continuing education meets an important need.

During the early stages of this crisis I was approached

about writing some books. This new challenge didn't remove the crisis, but it provided an opportunity for some personal therapy.

3. My physical body became a greater concern to me, and I began to watch more closely what I was eating. I also began to work more seriously on weight loss. I found that as I ate better food, lost some weight, and took a Stresstab (high-potency vitamin B complex) each day, I began to feel better about my physical body.

4. Change of scenery seemed to improve my spirits, even if only for a short period of time. Studying in California, conferences in Colorado, weekends away in the woods, and sailing all seemed to help lift my spirits. We are fortunate to have some friends who have loaned their recreational vehicles to us. It has been great to get out into the woods or go to the ocean, and to have a warm, dry place if it rained. The woods, the water, and sailing seemed to give me hope to make it through a few more days.

5. Music was significant during this crisis. At first, music played a depressive part. I listened constantly to the easy-listening stations, heavily oriented toward love songs. I was drawn to that kind of music, but the result was a deeper awareness that I was no longer a young man.

As the months went along, some music became extremely helpful to me. One of these songs was "Slow Down." I took it with me on tape one time to the woods and played it scores of times. It was as if God was massaging my heart through this song:

In the midst of my confusion,
In the time of desperate need,
When I'm thinking not too clearly,
A gentle voice does intercede.

Chorus:
Slow down, slow down,
Be still, be still and wait
On the Spirit of the Lord.
Slow down and hear his voice,
And know that he is God.

In the time of tribulation,
When I'm feeling so unsure,
When things are pressing in about me,
Comes a gentle voice, so still, so pure.*

6. Gradually I began to talk to Sally more openly about the pressures. At first she was threatened and frightened, so I wouldn't tell her much. But as the months went along, it was easier to share with her, even some of the things that were terribly damaging to her self-image. Each time we talked, I seemed to become freer, and in the following days our understanding and love for each other seemed to increase.

Most men I talk with are unwilling to share with their wives what they really feel. They are afraid they will blow the relationship apart. Strangely enough, most men feel that the relationship with their wife is bad and, at the same time, they want desperately to protect it.

7. Rest became important to me. During this time I came down with mononucleosis. I suppose I was physically exhausted and weak enough so that it hit me hard. As a result, I saw that I needed more rest and a more leisurely pace of life. I found I was totally burned out. The spark of creativity had disappeared.

"Just as the ocean ebbs and flows, man experiences

---

surges of creativity and effectiveness, followed by fallow periods when he needs regeneration. Our society rarely provides this opportunity. Work-obsessed Americans . . . must rediscover the meaning of leisure if they're to restore their creativity."[19]

American Christians have not really come to deal with leisure. They can't fully understand why God took a day off after he created the world. It certainly wasn't because God needed the rest; it was, rather, to set a pattern that our Protestant American work ethic has totally rejected.

Recently in one of our worship services a college girl shared what God taught her after she came down with mono this fall. She said, "I learned that what most glorified God was for me to rest and recover from the sickness. If I had tried to be up carrying out some Christian activity, I would have been out of God's will for me at that time. God is not so interested in what we do as in what we are."

As I saw my need for rest increasing during this time, I also found that I needed to be away from people. At first, this produced a great deal of guilt. After all, I was a people-helper. But I simply couldn't stand the emotional stress of people's problems. During the month of November I practically saw no one other than my family. I took no phone calls. I was in isolation for psychological recuperation.

8. I am fortunate to have several medical doctors in the church. These men have cared deeply for me and have ministered to me in more ways than physically. Their physical examinations gave me confidence that I was not soon to have a heart attack, and apparently there was nothing much wrong with my body other than mono and its effects. These men also spent time talking to me, asking about my emotional and spiritual life, encouraging me by saying I would make it through.

9. I came to a new understanding and appreciation of my mental health. Previously I had not done much to build my own mental health; I just assumed it would always be good and that I didn't need to bother about it. My attitude has changed. I know now that it is important for me to be spiritually and emotionally strong for my own benefit as well as for others. So, all of the things I have listed above are important for me to continue doing if I am going to be mentally healthy. I am also continuing to plan things for the future that will fit into the building of my mental health.

10. All through life I have spent time regularly reading the Bible and talking to God in prayer. This has not always been a daily routine and, increasingly, over the years I had spent more time looking for material to preach rather than going to the Scriptures for nourishment of my own soul.

Since my own mental health and spiritual well-being are important, I've come to see that spending an increased amount of time in the Bible and in prayer is vital. It is not taking hours away from my day and thus lowering my productivity, but this time with God contributes directly toward my ability to produce by keeping me spiritually and emotionally healthy.

The purpose of the Bible is to give us information about God and about ourselves. Hebrews 4:12 speaks about the Scriptures, "For whatever God says to us is full of living power: it is sharper than the sharpest dagger, cutting swift and deep into our innermost thoughts and desires with all their parts, exposing us for what we really are." 2 Timothy 3:16-17 adds, "The whole Bible was given to us by inspiration from God and is useful to teach us what is true and to make us realize what is wrong in our lives; it straightens us out and helps us do what is right. It is God's way of making us well prepared at every point, fully equipped to do good to everyone."

The quiet time alone with God is not a duty to impress God but is a vital necessity for my spiritual and emotional health.

THE KEY ROLE OF GOD

All of the above things were, beyond any question, useful and continue to be useful to move me through this mid-life crisis. The most significant person, however, during this entire time was God. His quiet ministry, through many of the things I did and through other people, was most significant. The subtle work of the Holy Spirit within my personality brought the greatest change in me.

Early in the crisis I became deeply aware that God was my ally. I could tell him anything, even share with him the contradictory motives within my personality, and he would still love and accept me. As the crisis deepened and I came into the depression and withdrawal stages, I knew intellectually that God was still my friend, even though I did not feel it emotionally.

During the early fall I preached a series of messages on the life of Daniel. The truth God kept bringing to my attention and I shared with the congregation was his miraculous sufficiency in all ages and all stresses of life. God continually confronted me with this truth; yet, at the same time, I did not *feel* that truth.

About nine months earlier God had led me to speak on the emotional and spiritual breakdown of Elijah as recorded in I Kings 19. It is the story of a prophet of God who came to the point of emotional and spiritual exhaustion and the special ministry of God to him.

I found in the story of Elijah some striking similarities to a man going through the mid-life crisis. Here was a man who had made a great spiritual impact and won a great victory over evil. As a result, his life was threatened. Earlier he might have stood his ground and fought. Now he was simply too tired, so "Elijah fled for his life" (v. 3).

Then we see that "he went on alone into the wilderness, traveling all day, and sat down under a broom bush and prayed that he might die" (v. 4). During the mid-life crisis a man often feels desperately alone, wondering what life is all about and even if it's worth continuing. I understood Elijah's death wish.

Elijah expressed self-pity. "I've had enough," he told the Lord. "Take away my life. I've got to die sometime, and it might as well be now" (v. 4).

God wasn't at all frustrated by Elijah's self-pity, but began to meet Elijah's needs. Ministering to his physical body was the first step. An angel brought food for him, and he went to sleep. The angel came again with more food in order to build up his body.

God's ministry continued by helping Elijah emotionally. He sent him on a long journey, which provided an opportunity for him to walk in the fresh air without responsibilities, to unwind for forty days and forty nights. God sent him to a new location, new scenery, a new place for refreshment.

Elijah was still feeling a great deal of self-pity when he said, "I have worked very hard for the Lord God of the heavens" (v. 10). Now God began to build Elijah spiritually. God revealed his power and grandeur—a demonstration to show his capability and his specific concern for the man in the cave. God asked, "Why are you here, Elijah?" (v. 13). He now began probing the deep spiritual questions—the reasons for man's existence, to whom does he owe allegiance, whom will he serve? In these moments as Elijah stood at the mouth of his cave, God in his gentle whisper was ministering quietly in the depths where no one else could touch.

God continued to build this man and bring him back into usefulness by telling him that he had a continued ministry for him. He was to anoint two kings as well as a new young prophet and prepare this young man for spiritual leadership in coming years.

God carefully ministered to all the dimensions of a man's life—physically with food and rest; emotionally with a freedom from responsibility and a change of scenery; spiritually with a quiet voice deep within. Finally, God ministered to a man's self-esteem and worth, showing him a continued useful ministry in the years to come.

The message from Elijah's emotional and spiritual breakdown is that God really cares for us and that crises through which we may go are just that—temporary crises in which we can count on the ministry of God from many different sources, so that we again become people who enjoy living and enjoy ministering.

THE RESULTS OF GOD'S WORK IN ME

In the beginning of this book I tried as honestly as possible to share my experience in the mid-life crisis, and I stopped on a very despondent note. Now I want to complete that story.

I had literally come to the end of my rope. During the previous months I had often felt very strong urges to simply go away from everything and everyone I knew. At that moment I was the lowest. I was ready to leave everything and run away for sure this time. I crawled into bed that November night and hardly slept as I made my plans. I was awake through most of the night, detailing specific steps I would take as I left my present life and ran away to start another life.

There were several discussions going on inside my mind. One part of me would ask, "Where are you going to go?"

The other part would answer, "Probably somewhere south where it's warm, to a small town near the ocean."

"And what will you do there?"

"I don't know; I'm willing to work at anything—anything just to make a little money to eat and to have a place to live."

"How do you know that everything will work out all right?"

"Well, God has always been faithful to me in the past; I'm sure I can depend on him in that new circumstance."

It was then that God quietly entered the conversation and said,

"If you can trust me to care for you when you run away to a new circumstance, why can't you trust me now to take you through this struggle without running away?"

There was a long silence.

All the voices were quiet in my mind. There was only a quiet reflection and a strange, new calm, and I soon dropped off to sleep, knowing that I had crossed a line into a new peace.

The next morning I spent some time reading the Bible, picking up where I had left off before, and God especially ministered to me.

In my distress I screamed to the Lord for his help. And he heard me from heaven; my cry reached his ears. . . .

He reached down from heaven and took me and drew me out of my great trials. He rescued me from deep waters. . . .

. . . You have turned on my light! The Lord my God has made my darkness turn to light. Now in your strength I can scale any wall, attack any troop. (Ps. 18:6, 16, 28-29)

I found myself saying with the Psalmist, "What a God he is! How perfect in every way! All his promises prove true. He is a shield for everyone who hides behind him" (18:30).

As the days went along, God continued his special ministry to me in my cave like Elijah. I began to sense that I had, in fact, turned a corner.

CHANGED SELF-IMAGE

Strangely now, the earlier self-pity was gone. I didn't seem to need that anymore. Now there was optimism. New goals seemed to be possible. I seemed to be thinking of myself as worthwhile and valuable, that I had a contribution to make to the lives of many people. I was far more valuable now at mid-life than I was when I was younger. Goals and ambitions began to move back into my personality. The future was no longer dreaded, but it seemed to be filled with opportunity.

I had a deep and pervading peace and, at the same time, a sensitive awareness of the loneliness in every human being. Part of me wanted to reach out and minister to every lonely person, yet the other part of me cautioned that I should let the healing process continue and not overextend myself. But I would never be the same again. I would more intensely feel the hurt and loneliness that every human being experiences.

Now a strange, new confidence has been growing. Fear seems to have faded into the background. That doesn't mean I am never afraid, but it seems now that my confidence in God has given me an assurance of continued usefulness all of my life, even though the type of usefulness may change. "One of the most amazing and heartening things about human beings is their capacity to change themselves and change their lives by altering their attitudes."[21]

It's only a nursery rhyme, but I have to smile now. Humpty Dumpty is together again. All the king's horses and all the king's men had nothing to do with it, of course, and it's not the same Humpty. I'm a new man—more mature, more understanding, more sensitive.

God had been working from many different directions, assisting me to change myself and changing me when I couldn't help myself. He had sent books, friends, a gracious wife and family, all with the purpose of moving me through the mid-life crisis to a new, settled, and productive era.

Saint Augustine summed it up when he said, "Our spirits are restless until they find their rest in God."[22]

> For who is God except our Lord? Who but he is as a rock?
> He fills me with strength and protects me wherever I go. (Ps. 18:31-32)

CHAPTER NOTES

CHAPTER 1

1. Barbara R. Fried, *The Middle-Age Crisis* (New York: Harper & Row, 1967), p. 7.

2. Peter Chew, *The Inner World of the Middle-Aged Man* (New York: Macmillan, 1976), p. 7.

3. Edmund Bergler, *The Revolt of the Middle-Aged Man* (New York: A. A. Wyn, 1954), p. 43.

4. Fried, p. 124.

5. Fred McMorrow, *Midolescence: The Dangerous Years* (New York: Quadrangle/New York Times, 1974), p. 63.

6. Eda J. LeShan, *The Wonderful Crisis of Middle Age* (New York: David McKay, 1973), p. 104.

7. D. B. Bromley, *The Psychology of Human Ageing* (Baltimore: Penguin, 1966), p. 13.

8. Joel and Lois Davitz, *Making It from Forty to Fifty* (New York: Random House, 1976), p. xvi.

CHAPTER 2

1. Kenn Rogers, "Mid-career Crisis," *Saturday Review of Society*, February, 1973, pp. 37-38.

2. Joseph Campbell, ed., R. F. C. Hull, trans., *The Portable Jung* (New York: Viking, 1971), pp. 12-13.

3. Davitz.

4. Fried.

5. Rogers.

6. Daniel Levinson, "The Normal Crises of the Middle Years," symposium sponsored by The Menninger Foundation at Hunter College, New York City, March 1, 1973, transcript, p. 9.

7. Gail Sheehy, *Passages* (New York: Dutton, 1976).

8. Maggie Scarf, "Husbands in Crisis," *McCall's*, June, 1972, vol. 99, no. 9, p. 76.

9. Fried, p. 7.

10. McMorrow, p. 38.

CHAPTER 4

1. Harry Levinson, *The Exceptional Executive* (Cambridge, Mass.: Harvard University Press, 1968), p. 79.

2. Peter F. Drucker, *The Age of Discontinuity* (New York: Harper & Row, 1968-69), p. x.

3. Kenneth Soddy and Mary C. Kidson, *Men in Middle Life* (Philadelphia: Lippincott, 1967), p. 238.

4. Soddy and Kidson, p. 238.

5. LeShan, pp. 15-16.

6. Robert A. Raines, "Middle-Agers Are Beautiful," *Lord, Could You Make It a Little Better?* (Waco: Word, 1972), p. 135. Used by permission of Word Books, Waco, Texas.

7. Margaret Mead, quoted in Martha Weinman Lear, "Is There a Male Menopause?" *The New York Times Magazine*, January 28, 1973.

8. Richard Knox Smith, *49 and Holding* (New York: Two Continents, 1975), p. 5.

9. Chew, p. 33.

10. Robert Lee and Marjorie Casebier, *The Spouse Gap* (Nashville: Abingdon, 1971), p. 64.

11. Anne W. Simon, *The New Years: A New Middle Age* (New York: Knopf, 1968), p. 34.

12. Scarf, p. 76.

CHAPTER 5

1. Fried, p. 59.
2. Fried, p. 59.

CHAPTER 7

1. Smiley Blanton, *Now or Never*, (Inglewood Cliffs, New Jersey: Prentice-Hall, 1959), p. 174.

2. Roger Barrett, *Depression—What It Is and What to Do About It* (Elgin, Ill.: David C. Cook, 1977), p. 9.

CHAPTER 8

1. Gloria Heidi, *Winning the Age Game* (Garden City, N.Y.: Doubleday, 1976), p. 7.

2. Joyce Brothers, *Better Than Ever* (New York: Simon & Schuster, 1975), pp. 19-20.

3. Brothers, p. 20.

4. Brothers, p. 20.

5. Berniece and Morton Hunt, *Prime Time*, (New York: Stein and Day, 1975), p. 164.

6. Davitz, p. 93.

7. Robert Manry, *Tinkerbelle* (New York: Harper & Row, 1965), p. 218.

8. Col. Edwin E. "Buzz" Aldrin, *Return to Earth* (New York: Random, 1973), pp. 308-309.

9. In "Male Menopause: The Pause That Perplexes," produced by National Public Affairs Center for Television (NPACT), original production June 24, 1974.

CHAPTER 9

1. Rust L. Hills, *How to Retire at Forty-One* (Garden City, N.Y.: Doubleday, 1973), p. 3.
2. Hills, p. 98.
3. Henry David Thoreau, as quoted by Hills, p. 122.

CHAPTER 10

1. Chew, p. 58.
2. Fried, p. 6.
3. Morton Hunt, *The Affair* (New York: New American Library, 1969), p. 29.
4. Fried, p. 41.
5. LeShan, p. 79.
6. Harry J. Johnson, *Executive Life-Styles* (New York: Crowell, 1974), p. 19.
7. Bergler, p. 164.
8. Sheehy, p. 471.
9. Chew, p. 72.

CHAPTER 11

1. Bernice and Morton Hunt, *Prime Time*, p. 93.
2. Judith Viorst, *How Did I Get to Be 40 and Other Atrocities* (New York: Simon & Schuster, 1973), p. 39.
3. David R. Mace, *Success in Marriage* (Nashville: Abingdon, 1958), p. 100.
4. Fried, p. 114.

CHAPTER

1. For an expanded treatment read Charlotte Buhler, "The Curve of Life as Studied in Biographies," *Journal of Applied Psychology*, 19 (1935), pp. 405-409; Walter Gruen, "A

Study of Erikson's Theory of Ego Development," Bernice Neugarten, ed., *Personality in Middle and Late Life* (New York: Atherton Press, 1964), pp. 2-3; and Daniel Levinson, *Seasons of a Man's Life* (New York: Knopf, 1978).

2. Sheehy, pp. 29-46.
3. Daniel Levinson, *Normal Crises*, p. 11.
4. Daniel Levinson, *Normal Crises*, pp. 11-12.
5. Wolfe, p. 160.
6. Daniel Levinson, *Normal Crises*, p. 14.

CHAPTER 14

1. Elisabeth Kübler-Ross, *On Death and Dying* (New York: Macmillan, 1969), pp. 38-137.

CHAPTER 15

1. Fried, p. 43.
2. Jane Price, *You're Not Too Old to Have a Baby* (New York: Farrar, Strauss & Giroux, 1977).
3. Fried, pp. 70-71.
4. Fried, p. 86.
5. Fried, p. 39.
6. Helen Van Slyke, "The Inescapable Threat of the Older Woman," *Harper's Bazaar*, August, 1973, vol. 106, p. 128.
7. Van Slyke, p. 128.

CHAPTER 16

1. Brothers, pp. 162-69.
2. James Dobson, *What Wives Wish Their Husbands Knew About Women* (Wheaton, Ill.: Tyndale, 1975), pp. 143-156.
3. Davitz, p. 198.
4. Sheehy, p. 337.
5. Viorst, p. 45.

CHAPTER 17

1. *Statistical Abstracts of U.S.*, U.S. Bureau of Census, 1976, table #97, p. 68. *Vital Statistics of the U.S.*, Public Health Service, 1973, vol. 1, table 1-11.

2. LeShan, pp. 148-149.

3. Lee, pp. 31-32.

4. Morton Hunt, *The Affair*, p. 288.

5. John Levy and Ruth Munroe, *The Happy Family* (New York: Knopf, 1940), p. 3.

6. Lee, p. 127.

7. Lillian E. Troll, *The Best Is Yet to Be–Maybe* (Monterey, Calif.: Brooks/Cole, 1973), p. 85.

8. David L. Cohn, *Love In America* (New York: Simon & Schuster, 1943), p. 86.

9. Lee, pp. 130-131.

10. Robert F. Winch, *Mate Selection* (New York: Harper, 1958).

11. McMorrow, p. 168.

CHAPTER 18

1. Daniel Goldstine and others, *The Dance-Away Lover* (New York: Morrow, 1977).

2. Lee, p. 40.

3. George R. Bach and Peter Wyden, *The Intimate Enemy* (New York: Morrow, 1969), p. 1.

CHAPTER 19

1. Ollie Pocs and others, "Is There Sex After 40?" *Psychology Today*, June, 1977, vol. 11, p. 54.

2. McMorrow, p. 13.

3. Bernice and Morton Hunt, *Prime Time*, p. 79.

4. Sheehy, p. 461.

5. Henry Still, *Surviving the Male Mid-Life Crisis* (New York: Crowell, 1977), pp. 82-83.

6. Stanley Frank, *The Sexually Active Man Past Forty* (New York: Macmillan, 1968), p. 74.

7. Still, p. 212.

8. Frank, p. 222.

9. Lee, p. 112.

10. Lee, p. 117.

CHAPTER 20

1. Smiley Blanton, *Now or Never* (Englewood Cliffs, N.J.: Prentice Hall, 1959), p. 85.

2. Lee, p. 140.

3. Blanton, p. 86.

4. Lee, p. 142.

5. Jermyn McCahan, NPACT.

6. Chew, p. 138.

7. Martha Weinman Lear, "Is There a Male Menopause?" *The New York Times Magazine*, January 28, 1973, p. 65.

8. LeShan, p. 80.

9. Arthur Miller, *Death of a Salesman* (New York: Viking, 1949), p. 82.

10. Tim LaHaye, *Understanding the Male Temperament* (Old Tappan, N.J.: Revell, 1977), pp. 168-169.

11. Bernice and Morton Hunt, *Prime Time*, p. 105.

12. Bernice and Morton Hunt, *Prime Time*, p. 106.

13. Richard Carelli, "Court Rules in Favor of Jet Pilot, 58," *The Champaign-Urbana News-Gazette*, November 29, 1977, p. A12.

14. Thomas C., Desmond, "America's Unknown Middle-Agers," *The New York Times Magazine*, July 29, 1956.

15. Smith, p. 58.

16. Robert Peterson, *New Life Begins at Forty* (New York: Trident, 1967), pp. 35-46, 48-89.

17. Rush Loving, Jr., "The Automobile Industry Has Lost Its Masculinity," *Fortune*, October, 1972, p. 190.

18. Richard Nelson Bolles, *What Color Is Your Parachute?* (San Francisco: Ten Speed, 1970; rev. 1977), pp. 68-69.

19. Bolles, p. 41.
20. Bolles, pp. 66-67.
21. John C. Crystal and Richard N. Bolles, *Where Do I Go From Here With My Life?* (New York: Seabury, 1974), p. 201.
22. Bernice and Morton Hunt, *Prime Time*, pp. 104, 108.
23. "Employment and Earnings," *Bureau of Labor Statistics*, vol. 24, no. 1, January, 1977.
24. LeShan, p. 90.
25. Peterson, p. 94.

CHAPTER 21

1. Bernice and Morton Hunt, *Prime Time*, p. 39.
2. Bernice and Morton Hunt, *Prime Time*, p. 38.
3. Desmond.
4. Bernice and Morton Hunt, *Prime Time*, p. 26.
5. Simon, pp. 167-168.
6. Chew, p. 128.

CHAPTER 22

1. Blanton, p. 70.
2. Chew, p. 76.
3. Bergler, p. 281.
4. Chew, p. 82.
5. Lulu Snyder Hamilton, *Your Rewarding Years* (New York: Bobbs-Merrill, 1955), pp. 88-89.

CHAPTER 23

1. LeShan, pp. 290-291.
2. Chew, p. 123.
3. Blanton, p. 236.
4. Ruth Shonle Cavan, "Family Tension Between the Old and the Middle-Aged," *Marriage and Family Living*, November, 1956, pp. 323-327.

5. Rose N. Franzblau, *The Middle Generation* (New York: Holt, 1971), pp. 228-229.

6. Cavan, p. 326.

7. LeShan, p. 275.

8. LeShan, pp. 275-276.

CHAPTER 24

1. Simon, pp. 72-73.

CHAPTER 25

1. Chew, p. 6.

2. Paul Tournier, *Learn to Grow Old* (New York: Harper & Row, 1972), p. 218.

3. Simon, p. 155.

4. Ernest Becker, *The Denial of Death* (New York: The Free Press, 1973), p. ix.

5. Simon, p. 217.

6. Rollo May, *Love and Will* (New York: Norton, 1969), p. 99.

CHAPTER 26

1. Scarf, p. 76.

2. Davitz, p. 59.

3. Davitz, pp. 61-62.

4. Bergler, p. 75.

5. Bergler, p. 301.

6. Lear, p. 65.

7. Anthony Pietropinto and Jacqueline Simenauer, "How Men Really Feel About Sex and Love," condensed from "Beyond the Male Myth," *Reader's Digest*, January, 1978, vol. 112, no. 669, pp. 83-86.

8. Estelle Fuchs, *The Second Season* (Garden City, N. Y.: Anchor/Doubleday, 1977), p. 31.

9. Bergler, p. 104.

10. Bergler, p. 104

11. Mace, p. 88.

12. Don Schanche, "What Happens—Emotionally and Physically—When a Man Reaches 40," *Touay's Health*, March, 1973, vol. 51, no. 3, p. 43

CHAPTER 27

1. Fried, p. 13.

2. Neugarten, pp. 16-19.

3. John A. B. McLeish, *The Ulyssean Adult–Creativity in the Middle and Later Years* (New York: McGraw-Hill Ryerson, 1976).

4. Davitz.

5. Fried, p. ix.

6. Chew, p. 13.

7. Sheehy, p. 405.

8. Rogers, p. 38.

9. Tournier, p. 93.

10. Sheehy, p. 364.

11. LeShan, p. 240.

12. Bernice and Morton Hunt, *Prime Time*, pp. 148, 151.

13. J. S. Slotkin, "Life Course in Middle Age," *Social Forces*, December, 1954, vol. 33, pp. 171-177.

14. Judith Viorst, "How Do You Know When You're 40?" *The New York Times Magazine*, February 6, 1977, p. 66.

15. Josephine Lowman, "Don't Think 'Middle Age,' " *The Champaign-Urbana News-Gazette*, September 13, 1977, p. 10-A.

16. Davis F. Matheny, "Is There Life After 40?" *Minneapolis Star*, September 24, 1977, pp. 8-9.

17 Bergler, p. 297.

18. Gerald B. Hall, "What Happens to the Man over Forty?" tape for Renewing Love Alumni Seminar, Annandale, Va., 1975.

19. Chew, p. 211.

20. Blanton, p. 4.

21. Smith, p. 136.